The Calling of all Callings

Terence John Wood

Published by Terence John Wood
Publishing partner: Paragon Publishing, Rothersthorpe
First published 2022

ISBN 978-1-78222-966-7

Book design, layout and production management by Into Print
www.intoprint.net
+44 (0)1604 832149

Dedication

This book is dedicated to all who have suffered mental illness.

All profits to be donated to mental health charities.

The greatest feeling of wellbeing is felt the day after the pain goes away.

Contents

Foreword

I have known Terry since 1978. I saw him every day at University. In all those 44 years I have never known him to say anything that is deliberately untrue. Of course, he has been wrong on occasion, but not deliberately. He has always been charitable, helpful, and entirely of good character. Annoyingly so sometimes. He has a strong moral compass and he always spoke out if he thought something was not right.

I visited him one evening on my way back from working in London in 2005. He was much quieter than usual. We went to the pub and he apologised for his slow and subdued responses which he put down to the medication he was taking. I had no idea he was taking medicine. He told me he was taking medicine for bi-polar. I had no idea what that was. Terry had always been a bit hyper. I just saw it as part of his character, his charm. I never thought of it as an illness. We had a good laugh and a lot of fun as many people do at University. I'm sure none of our friends thought anything was wrong.

I was in the area again a few weeks later and we went for a curry. He always liked a curry. Imagine my surprise when this time he told me he thought he was Jesus and had a model of a new religion. These appeared to be his absolutely honest beliefs. My first instinct was to dissuade him from this belief, but instead, I just listened. How could the logical engineer, with a Master's Degree be convinced he was Jesus? I found his argument difficult to criticise on logical grounds the first time he told me about it. I still have the napkin, covered in curry and a "new model of humanity." Of course I also pointed out a few flaws in claiming to be Jesus and Terry's view has developed over time.

I did my best to "cure" Terry but this is his view. It exists in his mind and is real to him. He has collected evidence over time to support his belief. He has compared his DNA to Jesus's DNA. He has read the bible to see what people say about the second coming to find the evidence there. He has looked at the things that happened in his life and how they support his view.

Terry is not the only one to claim to be Jesus. There are surprisingly many. It is quite common that people who claim to be Jesus are also bi-polar. I would love that the book is written from the perspective of a person looking at *why* he believes he is Jesus, or the next Messiah. Although Terry does know this, and hopes this book can help people with similar issues, he also believes he is Jesus and found it difficult to divorce himself from this view in his writing.

If you are reading because you have a similar Messiah belief, or if you know someone who has, then we both hope you find some comfort or understanding in this book. If you are reading because you are looking for a new spiritual leader then Terry would love to take up the challenge. If you are yourself a religious leader, or follow a religion, then bear in mind where this "earthly" description of spirituality comes from. Terry is not trying to supplant your God, just to understand where these feelings come from and to test the theory that he is the next Jesus. If you are a psychologist then you have another "case study." If you are reading out of general interest, I think there are also plenty of interesting issues raised about how brains work, and can sometimes malfunction, or maybe just function differently. But remember, there is always the possibility of Terry being correct. How would Jesus get treated today?

Terry's sense of humour comes over in the book and I hope you also take it in good humour. Remember though, that this is a true story and an earnest belief, which raises many issues rather than getting to the bottom of them. One issue is about financing some research into why the brain can begin to function in such an unusual way and create such a fervent belief. Perhaps the economics of doing such research means it will never be viable to understand the issue and find a solution because it would benefit so few people. This leads to the speculation of many would be Messiahs about why they think they are "the one". But most of all enjoy the book and take the time to put yourself in Terry's shoes; take the time to think about and explore the issues involved; and wonder, "what if Terry is right?"

Adrian Woods

Foreword
by Michael Parkinson (the other one).

Terry Wood writes about his mental health problems with refreshing honesty, he tells his readers what he feels and perhaps not what they want to read. So I suggest that you open your mind to some rather startling disclosures and opinions. Anyone who has suffered in a similar way to Terry will have their own demons to fight.

In the autobiographical section again, Terry is startlingly honest, particularly in his description of driving misadventures. He describes using his engineering skills to use cars that most of us would have condemned to the scrap heap.

He has been desperately unlucky in personal family life and describes the savage health problem that his Mother endured for well over twenty years. It must have been agony for Terry witnessing what she had to endure. The situation was not helped by the tragic reaction from his Father that left Terry as the sole source of comfort over that period of time.

When it comes to the description of education from boyhood to university I feel humbled to have been asked to write a forward to Terry's book because he is on a higher intellectual plane than I could ever be.

Descriptions of the jobs that Terry did are riddled with complex engineering terms that make me respect his achievements and admire his ability. He will give you, the reader, an opportunity to reflect on your own working life and the deal that fate has dealt you.

It could be that reading this book may throw some light on problems that have affected you throughout your life and may provide some ideas on how to deal with them.

Michael Parkinson

Acknowledgements

My profound thanks go to the *Lincolnshire Echo* for allowing me to include the photograph of Lincoln Cathedral.
Also, to Michael Parkinson (not that one) for his help in getting this book to publication and his foreword.
To Adrian and Sue Woods for their comments, encouragement and support.
To Cy Pettit for his suggestion of a foreword which tied the variously unrelated chapters together.
To all the other friends who read the original drafts and found it interesting and remained good friends afterwards.
To Avtar Kalsi for proof reading it for me who I new would do a good job.
To Richard Branson who encouraged me via a magazine article to go for my dreams.
These acknowledgements are not to say that they believe in my assertion of being the reincarnation of JC.

Introduction

This is my story, my mental illness or wellbeing and how it developed through an overwhelming feeling of love. This led to my developing a model of humanity. Many people experiencing this condition are ground breakers in their fields of expertise.

The model of humanity defines the kingdom of heaven as being a group of people that are high on love and is not a place where God lives along with the dead.

I believe the miracles in the New Testament have alternative explanations using love as the key to explain what actually happened.

Events following my overwhelming feeling of love may be explained as being beyond what we would normally experience or simply as coincidence. St John the divine in Revelations calls it *"being in the spirit"*. Revelations 1:10, 4:2, 17:3 and 21:10.

The first section of the book describes poignant events in my life history in an autobiography.

The second section, spiritual awakening, details some theories such as the psyche handshake with actual events. It is as if they were trials to test me for the correct response. Each chapter is a chronological diary of independent challenges. Almost bush tucker challenges! This is exemplified by another would be Jesus who saw me shadow boxing and decided to challenge another patient and came off second best; clearly he failed that test. They continue through a diagnosis of bipolar disorder despite the fact that I never went low except for a short period following failed attempts to bring about the kingdom of heaven by pushing myself as high as I possibly could, in the safe environment of a mental ward, to see if psychic energy would bring about the kingdom of heaven. When I read that the oxytocin hormone is the "love drug" I realised that this could be the cause of my feelings of love for the world and its peoples. With so many mentally ill people believing themselves to be Jesus surely it is because they are in the same state of mind that he was and it is only a matter of time until one of us is crowned. This is my story which I truly believe. When I first had the thought I was Jesus I made a promise to God that I would do my best if he so desired it of me.

I recognise that there are several types of love including brotherly love, sisterly love, love of an inanimate object and many more. The specific love I am experiencing is that generated by oxytocin.

Events in the Scottish Business Trip confirmed to me that I once was Jesus.

Section three develops my "model of humanity" which defines the Kingdom of Heaven and its opposite being Earthliness. Not everyone is destined for the kingdom of heaven but with oxytocin everyone may experience this love if they wish.

The purpose of my mission is to introduce you to the new heaven and earth as predicted in Revelations 21:1.

Section 1
Autobiography

Betty (Mum) and John Michael (Dad) Woods' wedding

1.

Childhood

My parents were of working class origins. My father was a foreman looking after upwards of 200 mainly female electronics production workers in an electronics factory. He was born in Yorkshire and was an indentured fitter. He was a good car mechanic unafraid to take on any task including stripping down an engine to grind in the valve seats. My mum was a housewife looking after me and the household. She was born in South Wales near the Gower peninsula. My dad was the spiritual one, my mum the Earthly one. My dad was a good ballroom dancer having achieved the gold certificate and won a couple of dance competition cups. They met at a dance in Rugby where they both worked in factories for the 1940-1945 war effort.

A few years after they married, baby Terry arrived.

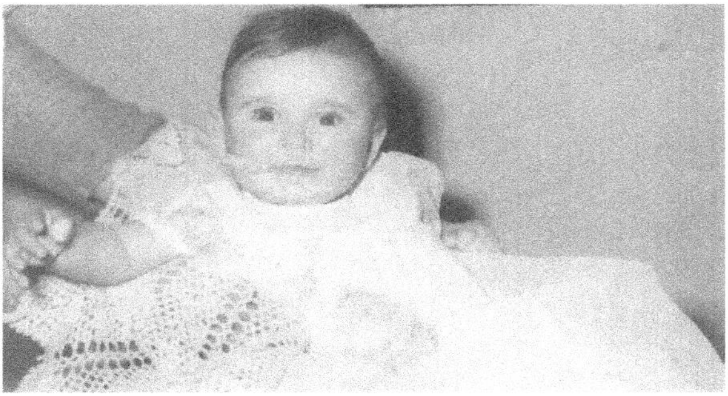

Terence John Wood as a baby

Dad in happier times
Top: Dad with his dance trophy in the background

I was an only child and all in all I had a happy childhood. I was a painfully shy child which I retained into adulthood especially when it came to the opposite sex. Even now into my latter years it takes time for me to get to know people. Maybe this is why I only have few but very good close friends.

My dad told me about a time before I could talk when I contracted acute diarrhoea. When I got near the kitchen I would scream loudly. My dad rearranged the furniture but still I wailed. He then took to carrying me round the room and every time I got near the kitchen sink I would scream louder, then my dad twigged that I wanted water as I was dehydrated!

Queuing for a mumps, rubella and measles injection made me afraid of needles. The next time we went and queued outside the hall I thought I'm not having this and screamed my head off. I wailed so much that they moved me to the front of the queue. When I got inside they gave me a sugar cube laced with the anti-polio serum. My fear of needles was compounded when I had a tetanus jab at secondary school when two nurses administered it. The first got me in a head lock with my arm twisted behind my back while the second nurse administered the vaccine. I got over my phobia at university when I had a course of 13 desensitisation injections.

2.

Junior School

In the very early years at junior school we were set the task of drawing a picture. My drawing depicted people whom I drew as stick men. The teacher held it up to ridicule it in front of the class and smacked me across the backside as punishment. When I told my mum she marched me down to see the teacher and told her off. I was pleased as punch. Then she said don't hit him across the rear, hit him on the legs, demonstrating even more painfully than the original reproach. Even to this day I am no good at drawing, and that includes technical drawing a requisite of my career in engineering.

One amusing occurrence at junior school was when a pot plant was sprayed silver. The headmaster demanded that the culprit own up. No-one did and so we were told the excursion to the pantomime would be foregone unless the culprit owned up. So the fall guy of the class admitted to the crime. The headmaster, after interrogating the lad at length, announced to the class that he was certain he did not do it. Ultimately it turned out that it was the class cleaner's young daughter who did it. So we got to go to the pantomime after all.

I remember one occasion when I tore a new coat and afraid of the punishment I would receive from my parents I blamed the previously mentioned fall guy. I thought that would be the end of it but my mum found out where he and his parents lived and went there to remonstrate. Can't remember the consequences only that years later I worked with the lad's father and he confronted me with it. I stayed quiet not remembering the incident until sometime later. I should have craved his and his son's forgiveness but never did. I learnt my lesson about lying and to this day I do not lie unless it is tongue in cheek – my memory and spontaneity is not sufficient to react to the consequences of the snowballing effect of the lie getting bigger and bigger.

3.

Grammar School

I marginally passed my 11+ and qualified for grammar school where I entered the mid-stream. I was teased remorselessly about my surname which I took to heart until the day I caught a tormentor with the intention of giving him a good hiding until he said he was no longer playing. To me it was not a game. From that day on I went along with it and just let the teasing wash over me. I was over sensitive but given my future destiny, to me, a sleight on my name was serious. One of my village schoolmates rewrote the lyrics to the song entitled a wandering star by Lee Marvin which hurt badly and to this day I do not like the song.

Speaking of sensitivity, I suffered terribly from hay fever. Every summer my eyes would stream and I would sneeze for England. It didn't help that we lived next to an unkempt field. This didn't help with my education. I had sensitisation tests whereupon I was pricked with allergens up my arm and I reacted to all of them – grass pollens, tree pollens, cat fur, dog fur you name it I was allergic to it. Fortunately I was not allergic to food stuffs which have been fatal to some of those affected.

One day in the summer holidays my dad had an old TV cathode ray tube for disposal. We decided to implode it. So at a safe distance we fired air rifle pellets at the front of it. It resisted so I threw stones at it from a closer range with no effect. So I progressed to rocks at an even closer distance. At last it imploded. After it blew and the vacuum had pulled the fragments of glass inward, it exploded outwards and shards of glass embedded the shed and fence behind us. Both me and my dad, who was behind and to the right of me, escaped uninjured. Either God or being in the protective shadow of the rock saved us.

My earliest work experience was when I was 13 or 14 when I got special dispensation from the council to work in the same factory as my dad during the summer holidays in the outgoing stores department. One of the duties was to shred waste paper used to pack outgoing products. I gradually increased the number of sheets shredded at once until the machine finally said that's enough and conked out. The maintenance department found an internal fuse that had blown which the maintenance electricians were not previously aware of. Another task was nutting. This entailed taking a tray of diodes and screwing nuts onto the threads. This was boring and made my hands sore. To alleviate the boredom I would make intricate patterns in both trays by way of removing diodes from the array in the yet to do tray and also when returning the finished product in the completed product tray.

Later in my late teens I was given a desensitisation course of Alvac P. As I recall. It was a 10 week course but if you reacted to an injection the course had to be aborted. I had heard that recipients who reacted violently had died. Needless to say three weeks in I reacted to one. Rather than stop the course they repeated a dose. It worked. A 10 week course turned into 13 weeks after repeated doses. But it was well worth it. After the treatment summer was no longer to be feared. To this day I am still allergic to duck down and have to be careful about bedding.

The teachers at the school were in the main exemplary.

The French teacher used to scour the class and descend on a pupil that failed to understand, me included I am proud to say and used to massage the back of one's head and say he was exorcising the "fagascites". To this day no one knows what a fagascite is. Another teacher on his first lesson silently assessed the class and roamed the class stopping behind the main troublemaker and whacking him so hard with a voluminous book behind the head that he bent over and hit his head on the desk in front. He was one of the best teachers we had. In comparison we had a physics teacher that plainly knew is subject but couldn't teach for toffee. Not only that, but he couldn't maintain class discipline. Even when I thought that I needed to pass his subject to qualify for my apprenticeship I couldn't understand his teaching.

It was half way through my secondary education when I found I could not fight. My arms and in particular my wrists were and are very small for a male. They are typically half the size of the average man. For many years I was self-conscious about them and would always wear long sleeved shirts buttoned to the hand. As I matured I accepted them and no-one took any notice anyway. As a consequence there is no force if I punch any-one – a powder puff puncher I think they call it or put another way I was gentle as a lamb. If I am faced with trouble my legs go to jelly and I have to talk my way out of the situation. One time in school I got into a fight with a classmate and he had me in a headlock and was punching me hard. I was trying to prick his conscience by telling him that he was picking on someone that couldn't fight back. He eventually let go and caught me with haymaker of a right hand that made me go dizzy for a few moments and then it was all over. So there you have it I have no choice other than to be a pacifist. I do not begrudge others who wish to fight and am grateful to the armed forces for keeping us free and safe but believe there is mostly a passive solution to conflict or ultimately accept the things you cannot change.

I was not a good sportsman although I later became proficient at badminton and my favourite sport was pool. As a youngster I loved football and was always kicking a mostly burst football after school. I was too shy to push myself forward for the Tennyson house football team and was probably not good enough anyway. There was a defender that went on to play for Leicester City and England under 21s. He used to command the whole of the defensive half of the pitch, and so they never needed to improve the squad anyway. My favourite position was goalkeeper. Then a more strict games master came to the school and some of our year of the Saxilby contingent – six of us would bunk off school. Then they built a swimming pool and I loved swimming so suddenly there was this new student. The pool was supposed to be of Olympic standard or so we thought but when it opened it was too small and the last third of the shallow end was so shallow that your knees hit the bottom of the pool when trying to breaststroke a length.

Once a year we would go to the cathedral for a religious service. When the service was over we would run down Steep Hill which is one of the steepest inhabited hills in the country, trying to catch the early bus home. Woe betide the pedestrians that we had to negotiate around with school bags aside of us.

In my final year at school we had a free period and someone produced a pack of cards. I can't recall what we played but I do remember it was for a penny a hand. I think it may have been pontoon. I vividly recall losing hand after hand. As the end of the period neared I played double or quits on cutting the pack for red or black. Still I kept on losing. Eventually the class ended with me owing in the order of £10 – a small fortune to a lad whose pocket money was just 5p a week. I don't think I ever did clear the debt but if the lad I owe the money to wants to claim it I will gladly pay up with a 5% per year increase to compensate for inflation. It taught me a lesson not to gamble and barring a tote on the Grand National or a bus stop card which is a card of twenty football teams which cost a pound each to select a hidden team which is revealed when the card is full. Half the proceeds go to the person who chose the winning team and half to the landlord to pay for an evening's supper. I have never seriously gambled since. I do not see the harm in putting a small wager on a sports event to add interest in the outcome but I do not recommend chasing your losses. I recall the lad I played cards with that day was a relatively short lad and I met him in Lincoln a few years after we had left school and he must have had a massive growth spurt for he was now over 6 foot tall.

Later in life on a Caribbean cruise the liner gave £10 in tokens to gamble with in the casino. The first week I passed up the chance to gamble but in the second week I thought I would just convert the chips to redeemable moneyed chips. So, on the roulette table I put the gifted chips equally on the red black and green sectors. On converting the chips I watched the gaming table for some time. There was an indicator above the table which told you the last several numbers which had come up. If the last three numbers were black I would punt on red and progressed to covering four numbers in a sector that hadn't come up recently. Based on this I gambled some of my chips. I would then wait again for similar sequenced betting. I did well earning a 300% increase on my initial stake. Then I suffered a total wipe out. I lost all the chips I had placed on the gaming table for that spin of the wheel. So I cashed in what chips I had and still made 200% profit. I was later told that the indicator had not been working properly so my win was based on pure luck rather than probability. I recounted the tale to fellow passengers and one was the cruise comedian. He was impressed with the return and asked me how much I had made. £20 I told him. Don't know if he recounted the tale on stage!

I watched an American on the pontoon table lose £700 in less than 10 minutes. After that I walked away in case I was somehow jinxing him.

I was an average student having gained four out of eight 'O' levels of marginal pass grades apart from maths which, fostering a belief that I was good at it from an early age, encouraged success. This was belied from the fact that the answers were in the back of the text book at Junior school and looking back at old work books it was obvious I didn't understand the workings at that early age.

I left school at 16 with just enough qualifications to embark on an electrical technician's apprenticeship.

4.

Apprenticeship

The first year of my apprenticeship was spent at Ruston's training school. There we learnt manual tool skills, machining expertise on lathes, milling machines, shapers and the like and a spell on electrical installation.

As a sensitive individual I was very ticklish. Now this may not sound important but when one of your soon to become best friends finds out and decides to assail you from behind when you're operating a lathe or milling machine the danger becomes apparent. On one occasion I was using a micrometre to measure the diameter of a turned steel rod when my friend assailed me from behind. I reacted accordingly and when he had desisted set the lathe in motion with the micrometre still in situe. The micrometre was bent way beyond recovery. My apprentice friends rallied behind me and returned the broken instrument without admission of liability. If appropriation is required I will gladly reimburse the company for a new micrometre all these years later.

I remember vividly that there was a girl that I really fancied who used to walk through the workshop. I used to see her in the canteen too. My friends would always egg me on to ask her out. But every time I approached her words would fail me. My language turned to gobbldygook and I would make a hasty exit. Many years later I saw her in a street in Lincoln with a hunk of a guy and his child.

The next two years were spent in my employer's factory

– AEI in various departments including the drawing office where I had to draw a centrifugal silicon slice acid etching jig. This was a nightmare. Given my inability at technical drawing I struggled for weeks to get it right. It was a circular rotational jig that had slots for the wafers at oblique angles in the body. Try as I may it took for ever to get the darned drawing right.

The other thing I remember was cleaning the draughtsmen boards with trichloethelyn. Not good for the lungs.

We used to frequent Ruston's club in unity square where my mum and dad used to participate in the Saturday night ballroom dances. Meanwhile I was gaining experience on the pool table downstairs. One time I remember getting absolutely sozzled on lager and lime with rum and black chasers with my apprentice friends. My dad came to take me home and my friends scattered. He carried me down the stairs under his arm and as we walked to the car along Monks road a police car drove past and we were swaying as if both drunk and my dad said act sober you fool as I wasn't legally old enough to drink alcohol. That night I spoke to God down the big white telephone and when I was put to bed the ceiling spun round.

Another year was spent in the diode production department where principally I tested pilot batches of diodes to ensure they met quality standards before larger production runs went through. I was the first person to set fire to a diode when a test button got stuck in on a power test station. This was the first time I was exposed to girls as the majority of the workforce were women and I dated a few.

The good friend that I mentioned earlier passed his driving test at the third attempt but well before me and bought a mini-van. He would call for me of a Sunday and we would tour Lincolnshire often going to Skegness for the day, sometimes with our then girlfriends. Later he would marry his girlfriend for which I was his very nervy best man.

At technical college I excelled at academia. The first year I was put on the T1 (year 1 technician) course which was effectively a repeat of my schooling. I also retook my English language O level at night school which as it turned out was essential for advancement to my next place of study. I gained good grades and was promoted to study a day release ONC (Ordinary National Certificate) and on to the second year of a block release OND (Ordinary National Diploma). I again excelled achieving distinctions and credits throughout my subjects. So much so that on completion of my OND in the third year of my apprenticeship, I was eligible for university.

Meanwhile back at the ranch they had developed the field next to our bungalow into a new junior school. This was always on the cards which my parents knew about before buying the property. Despite this they went ahead and bought the bungalow. However, the developers changed the plans to put the playground next to our property. All went well for a few years. We even played a football game called wall ball. The aim was to kick the football at a wall with the aim of preventing the oncoming player from hitting the wall. Also we played bike football on the playground. This was mainly in the evenings after school homework and later after leaving school in my latter teenage years.

During my 17th year mischievous night came along. This is November 4th, the day before Guy Fawkes Night. A gang of youths led by an elder youth and my ex-school friends saw it fit to attack our bungalow from the playground. But it didn't stop at mischievous night and our bungalow was under siege night after night. The police became involved but the only miscreants they caught were me and the headmaster's son walking round the school one day. We got a ticking off but were let off. It got on my dad's nerves so much that on one night he vaulted the wall at the front of the property over a fifteen foot drop to the playground below and chased after the youths with a newly sprained ankle. I joined the chase careful not to catch anyone. My dad was after the ring leader but he and the rest of them hurtled across the field and over the fence into the Recreation ground and away. Needless to say this increased the taunting to such an extent that just before my 18th birthday we sold up and moved to an exclusive village to the east of the city. Just when I was nearly old enough frequent the four pubs in that old village, we moved to a dry village.

5.

Learning To Drive

In the main my dad taught me to drive. Prior to my 17th birthday he had taken me to Wigsley's aerodrome and let me drive up and down the disused runways avoiding the remote control model aeroplane enthusiasts and their boys' toys.

On my 17th birthday my provisional license arrived and we began earnestly on the roads.

Originally I couldn't stop weaving from side to side. He mentioned this to a colleague at work who told him to tell me to look further forward into the distance which did the trick.

Driving back from my Aunt and Uncles house at Leicester we were travelling back along the A46 with the setting sun in my eyes. Motorbikes were heading home from a Cadwell Park meeting in the opposite direction with headlights blazing and overtaking in the middle of the road at every opportunity. By the time we got to Lincoln I was relieved and relaxed. I took the south park roundabout exit to go down the high street and there was a pedestrian on a Zebra crossing that I just didn't see. My dad hollered and pulled on the handbrake and I reacted too. It was a near miss and a valuable lesson in maintaining concentration at all times.

I took a few professional lessons and told my dad he was teaching me all wrong at which he was most offended and told me so. So I went back to him to teach me further.

The professional tutor did teach me a few things which were of use. Like visualising where the offside back wheel was when reversing into a parking space.

I failed my first test on a few points and didn't reapply for a re-take for a few weeks. The day of the second test came along and the Cortina was backfiring. My dad spoke to the examiner and explained that he hadn't had time to fix it. The examiner didn't seem to mind and we set off. The first time the car backfired I looked at him in horror but he remained expressionless. The car behaved itself after that. Then came the time for the emergency stop. I applied the footbrake and yanked the handbrake, as my dad had taught me, and we safely came to a halt. The examiner said "shall we do it properly now?" I said "I have done it properly." He said "you don't apply the handbrake and just use the footbrake." So I did it again his way. Well, that's it I thought – another failure. When the test was completed the examiner said to me "on which wheels are the brakes activated when the foot pedal is operated?" "All four" I said. "Which wheels brake when you operate the handbrake?" he asked. "Rear" I said and the examiner stayed quiet." "Front" I blurted, "no rear". Ultimately he confirmed that it was the rear and said "what is the point of operating the hand brake when the footbrake activates all four wheels? Besides" he said, "you need both hands on the steering wheel in an emergency." Then he turned to me and said "I'm pleased to say you have passed." "You're *kidding*" I said and quickly shut up.

Later that day my dad let me take the car out on my own for the first time and I drove it for the first 600 yards with the handbrake on!! Good job I didn't do that in the test.

Some months later I borrowed my dad's car in the lunch hour to go up town. Inching it into the multi storey parking space with the philosophy that it will fit, I nudged the pillar. I knew it was bad from the expression of a passing lady. Arriving back at work I surveyed the damage and there was a big indentation in the passenger's door. I went to tell my dad. He was quite understanding about the prang. When we got home he removed the interior fixtures of the door and gave the indent a whack with a hammer. Twang it went and the indentation came out with a small mark where the hammer had struck. Lesson learnt – never assume the car will fit into a space.

It would be another 5 years before I owned my first car.

6.

Loughborough University Of Technology

I was accepted at Loughborough University of Technology to study Electrical and Electronic engineering. The jump from OND to undergraduate was too great. I went from being a big fish in a small pond to being a small fish in a big ocean. This is despite having had extra maths tuition after my OND at Tech College to bring me up to speed with differentiation and integration. I should have gone on to take my HND (Higher National Diploma) before embarking on a degree. But this would have meant adding two more years to my academic career, and 19 was a good age to go to higher education. The tech college learning was not so intense. It offered bite size chunks of new learning. Nottingham University offered me a place conditional of doing a preliminary year there. This would have been a better option. Not only would it have given me a better grounding for the degree but the ratio of men to women there was far more favourable than the engineering based Loughborough contingent.

The only time I was up to date with my studies was the on the first day of the course, such was the volume of information I was inundated with. I was billeted to Hazlerigg Rutland hall of residence affectionately known as RiggRut on the campus – an all-male hall. Struggling with my studies and being shy I was very lonely. Thank goodness for the darts and snooker matches. The inter hall darts league was played in the local pubs which I relished.

Every weekend I would travel back home by train, which didn't help with the academic workload.

The Freshers at the hall of residence were ignominiously, one by one, dumped in the fountain by the seniors. The day came when it was my turn – A knock came on my door and on answering I was confronted by numerous seniors. I was hauled to the ground and carried out to the fountain. I didn't escape. It was futile to struggle.

That damned fountain as viewed from RiggRut

Somehow I passed enough of the modules to allow me to progress to the second year. I was able to drop some of the subjects I was less strong at and I put more effort into the maths module. One topic I excelled at with little effort was control theory. I loved it. Should have pursued a career in it but accepted what came along after my degree to stay local to Lincoln and my parents.

Socially I was fitting in better now having met what

would be a lifelong good friend who got the room I had reserved due to a mix up with our similar surnames. We used to frequent the local town pubs usually later in the evenings after some homework. On one occasion we downed 5 or 6 Carlsberg Specials within an hour in the Warwick arms pub. When I got back to the campus I couldn't walk. I had to run so that the momentum kept me going in a straightish line. It is the only time I have been unable to get out of bed to be sick. I could have died that night by choking on my own vomit. My friend brought egg and chips and left it outside my door. It goes without saying that I didn't eat it. Needless to say I missed lectures the next day with a sore head.

Sometime after I left school I sought help for a shortage of breath especially when exercising and was diagnosed as having asthma. I had to use a Ventolin inhaler. I discovered barn dancing and took a shine to it, particularly as girls were involved. But it was very energetic and on one occasion I forgot to take my inhaler with me and suffered an asthma attack. Your windpipe closes up and you produce an excess of thick mucus and you can't get air into your lungs. I imagine it's like you are drowning but away from water. So steadily I walked back to my room where the inhaler was, but it was empty. Suck as I may on my puffer I could not get relief. I eventually gave up and concentrated on slowing my breathing and to stop panicking. Eventually I fell asleep and woke the next day with the attack over. I could have died again that night – people have died of asthma attacks. Frightening!

Having travelled back one Sunday night I was summoned to the student bar where an inter hall of residence sing song was taking place. At the end of the night someone threw a glass into the middle of the gathering onto the stone floor.

Suddenly everyone barring me threw their glasses – I still had beer in my glass. The bar manager stood in the middle of the maelstrom with glass flying all about him. After that the bar only ever used plastic glasses. Reckless really!

During rag week, a time for high jinx to raise money for charity, sponsorship was raised to see our economics lecturer custard pied during his lecture. On the fateful day four burly students descended the two walkways to the lecture podium. There was no escape. As I recall one of the assailants slipped on the way down the aisle but balanced the two plates of shaving foam without spilling them. Then the lecturer was pied. He did not take it well. He sued the students union claiming his leather jacket was ruined. He refused to lecture us anymore. I did feel sorry for him as he was pied and was sorry not to have him finish his course as I quite liked economics. The incident was even reported in the national press.

On my route back to the hall of residence on a Sunday night my treat was a beer in an old fogy's pub. Hearsay has it that a trilogy of Rag week students went into this pub and asked for half of beer and when the barman came back they asked for three straws and were duly shown the door.

In a previous year the mountaineering club pasted cut-out feet as if a giant was climbing a high rise building on campus. The powers that be made them remove the footprints but the white glue remained to remind following years' students of the prank.

And so to the final year. My previous philosophy was to attend all the lectures, get the information then gain the understanding when doing the final cramming before the exams so that it was fresh in my mind. We had to complete a final year project which counted towards 20% of the final mark. I chose to do a distributed thick film based project which entailed writing off to paste manufacturers for samples of their wares. Several responded and I set about screen printing, oven firing and testing the finished circuits to produce graphs of their performance. All of this took time and effort which took me away from my academic studies. The production of the very thick final thesis was also laborious and took all of my time up. I am grateful to two typists at work who labelled the numerous graphs and titled them for me. But the fact remained that I had to do the assimilation of the final reports. It had to be done otherwise all the previous work would count for nothing. I knew I was running out of time for cramming for the exams. In the hall of residence the song Suicide is painless by Johnny Mandel – the theme music to M.A.S.H. wafted into my room on a regular basis. I was told I was awarded an A for the project but it was at the expense of the exams. In the exams I just couldn't answer the questions. It was the first time I spent the duration of the exams looking around at my fellow students beavering away.

Needless to say I did not succeed, but rather than fail me, so I could resit the final year, they awarded me a very rare degree. A BSc hons ungraded pass degree which did not entitle me to use the hons title after the BSc despite studying the honours course. But there it was I had at least graduated. The lesson I would offer to future students is to choose a project of modest complexity.

My hall mates were always surprised at the end of each term when my dad would turn up in the old style smaller mini and the whole contents of my room would be squeezed into the car along with me, my dad and maybe even my mum too!

7.

Nottingham University

A few years into my working career the opportunity arose for me to study an MSc in modern electronics by day release at Nottingham University. It was a modular course with 12 examinable modules and a project to do at the end of the course. The first two modules came and I failed them both. This is the end of my academic career I thought but my mum gave me a kick up the backside and I carried on, passing the next four modules. Rather than reading round the subject, I was now regurgitating the material the lecturers had taught me and it seemed to work.

I couldn't progress to the second year until I had passed the two failed modules and so had a year off to re-sit the two modules, which I duly did. It was a blessing that I had the year off as I had to contend with my mother's stomach cancer and my father's suicide in that year.

At the end of the first year I arranged to go on a pub crawl around York with a chap I had met on the course and had gelled well with as a partner on the practical assignments. It was particularly convenient in that my then girlfriend's parents lived in a village near York and so she drove. I got absolutely bladdered but my friend was not drinking which I didn't think anything particularly odd at the time. When we got to the hotel we were staying at he had booked a twin room. Still I didn't twig. Then I perceived that he had made a pass at me and I said I'm sorry but I'm not homosexual and he said he wasn't gay either but a blazing row ensued and I thought I'm out of here so repacked my case and left. Staggering through the streets of York I came across a couple of policemen and asked them if they knew of a cheap and cheerful hotel. They didn't arrest me but pointed out an appropriate hotel. I booked in, went to my room and got undressed down to my underpants ready for bed when I thought I need a pee. So went down the corridor to the toilet. On returning to my room the door was shut and the key was inside the locked room. I went down to reception for the master key only to be told it was with the manager who would not be in until after dawn. So I hunkered down with a blanket on the cloth sofa in the reception area for a terrible night's sleep. To the best of my recollection no-one else came into the hotel before the man with the master key arrived early next morning. My word did my head hurt the next day! I went back to the original hotel to meet my girlfriend as arranged and overheard two guests saying "did you hear that argument late last night" … me! My friend had apparently driven home immediately after the altercation.

The second year came around and I passed the remaining modules. I was so determined to pass the latter modules that when the exams were imminent I would go to the factory for a normal working day, come home, have my tea, go to bed at 6pm, get up at 10.30pm study throughout the night with a jug of filter coffee to keep me going then go to work the next morning at the normal time. Then repeat it until the exams came round.

And so on to the project. This was a more modest affair modelling a single pin oscillator on a computer aided design platform called Spice. I entered the circuit and ran the program overnight. Bingo, next day a 560kHz waveform appeared on the printout. Job done, just had to write it up now. But what would happen if I ran the simulation with the resonator disconnected? The self-same waveform materialised. How the hell was I to explain this away? I ultimately blamed it on free resonance.

I had done it a grade C (and almost a grade B) MSc. This was the equivalent of a Desmond BSc honours … a two two. My demons had been put to bed and I had avenged my first degree failure.

Above: Official graduation picture Nottingham University

Mum and I (left) and me (above left) in graduation robes in my aunt's garden

8.

Career

8.1. GEC /Marconi

After my first degree I went to work in the microwave department, manufacturing testing and trimming the frequency response of thick film IF amplifiers with a laser. The difference between my University project and this being that these amplifiers had discrete components soldered onto the thick film substrate. With the university project the substrate was the circuit itself without any components. All went well for the first few months until one day the frequency response was no longer right. I tried everything to put it right … changing all the components, laser trimming one malfunctioning circuit to within a whisker of an open circuit but nothing worked. Eventually weeks later I managed to borrow a capacitance bridge from another department and within 10 minutes I had it. The 100nF decoupling capacitors were the wrong value, all of them. They were all 100pF which meant they were 1000 times more conductive than they should have been and they were conducting some of the signal to earth thus decreasing the amplitude of the signal. Eureka. But it was too late to save my involvement with the project. I had to hand it over to a more experienced engineer and I was moved onto a new project. All I needed was the advice of an experienced Engineer.

The second project yielded another problem. This

time the surface mount capacitors were cracking when the circuit was subject to temperature cycling of -25 degree C to +125 degree C. It turned out that the difference in coefficients of expansion between the component and the solder was mismatched. The solution was to replace the standard lead tin solder with indium gallium solder – just on these rogue capacitors. It worked and I had solved the riddle fast enough to retain the project this time.

Later I moved onto making microwave amplifiers. One incident of note is worth recounting. We used to temperature cycle the circuits using either liquid nitrogen which came in stainless steel ewers resembling Daleks or liquid nitrogen cylinders. On this occasion I needed a liquid nitrogen cylinder which were slender and 6 foot tall. I got the old bespoke sack barrow, loaded one cylinder leaving the second place empty and fastened the safety chain. Walking the cylinder it squeaked loudly and one of the managers was on the phone in his office. He gave me a dirty look so I decided to park up and wait for him to finish his call. Levering the sack barrow up to the rest position the cylinder went past 90 degrees, kept going with the safety chain unravelling. So rather than save it the cylinder fell to the floor just catching the tap at the top of the cylinder against an object, probably a bench and the tap turned on hissing escaping gas. The manager in the office who was a Territorial Army reserve, with mitts as big as banana hands, dived under his desk. I stood open mouthed behind the back of the sack barrow unable to do anything but watch the cylinder topple over. Another engineer who saw what had happened jumped to action straddling the cylinder and turned off the tap. My hero! The sack barrow was not designed to take one cylinder. It had to take two cylinders so there wasn't any slack in the safety chain. But how was I to know before the accident? The cylinder was sent off to be X-rayed to make sure its integrity hadn't been compromised.

I made a good friend, with whom I have recently renewed contact, and we talked over religious ideas. We regularly worked in excess of 100 hour weeks to meet production demands. We used to go to the Royal Oak pub at Auborn of a Friday and weekends for a couple of beers and something to eat. I seem to remember one evening we walked the local three village circuit near my home with a couple of beers in each of the locals, chewing the cud as we walked.

A new manager was put over me with whom I did not get on with. An opportunity arose to transfer departments to the IC division as a telecoms telephone dialler chip and system X exchange chip applications engineer responsible for running development projects, verification of correct prototype operation and support for customers in the field.

I had some degree of success here having designed and built a piece of test equipment to test loop disconnect and DTMF dialler chips. Next I designed and build a circuit board to verify the operation of a System X frame aligner chip. My best design achievement everrr.

The department went for a Christmas meal at the Cross Keys at Stow and I had a most enjoyable meal in good company. The next morning my mum woke me early on saying that she could smell gas. So convincing was she that I called the emergency gas line. The Engineer arrived and on opening the door he said he could smell it but that it wasn't gas. Later on in the day I was at the shoulder of my mum and she said that smell was coming from me. It was the garlic mushrooms I had had the night before!

One of the training exercises was to make a presentation and deliver it in front of an audience with it being videoed. I am not a consummate orator – too conscientious of not portraying my true self character. My memory fails to recall what the presentation was about but it may have been my favourite sport of pool. That aside someone asked me a technical question that I simply couldn't answer. Again I can't recall the question. After what seemed at least 5 minutes, I thought I have to say something and so answered the question whilst thinking what a predicament I was in. I simply didn't know what I was saying. On seeing the video back the elapsed time was just a natural thinking break and the answer was most plausible.

My next encounter with garlic was in Malta. The night before I was due to fly back I asked the concierge what the local dish was. He told me it was rabbit stew. Most enjoyable it was too. The next morning I felt ill. In the queue to board the plane a fellow traveller said that I had been eating garlic!

I went on a camping holiday around France with my good friend from Loughborough University his cousin and girlfriend. My dad had told me look out for the drink chartreuse in the bars. I think it was in the Loire where we walked from the campsite to a small village and found the local tavern. No chartreuse but a German tourist told me to try the brandy from the dusty bottle at the back of the top shelf. So I asked the barman for it. He pointed to a bottle and I said "non, the one at the back." He finally got it and asked how many I wanted." "Four" I said and he said "vous desire quatre." " Oui" I said holding up four fingers. He poured them and asked for £20. That was a quarter of my holiday's spending money. But by heck was it good! We walked back to the campsite in pitch black darkness. Eventually we returned to England still not having found this elusive chartreuse but the first bar we went in in England had a bottle of green chartreuse behind the bar. It is a real fire water of a liqueur. Yellow chartreuse is also available.

Socially I set up a pool team in my local pub and I won the Lincoln and district singles championship in the first season we played. It was a bit of a double edged sword as pool players then knew my name but I hadn't a clue of theirs. It prepared me for meeting strangers.

Collecting my pool trophies with my good friend Adrian Woods

I went on to captain a Lincoln team in a county wide league, was a member of the Lincolnshire A and B sides for several years ultimately winning the B league championship at the finals in Yarmouth although I was not selected to play in the final, much to my disappointment. The year after I won the singles, I went out in the last 32. In the pub shortly afterwards a lady member of the team and her brother were in the pub and I asked if they would like to know how I had lost. She hesitantly said ok knowing that watching pool matches was boring enough let alone listening to recounts. So I raised my hands ready to gesticulate as to the position of the balls and said basically I fucked it up, much to her shock and amusement in equal measures as I very rarely swear.

I met a guy from the outset of setting up the pool team who went on to be a very good friend. We would alternately drive on a Saturday night to tour Lincolnshire visiting the pubs. We eventually found our favourite at the Black Horse in Ludford where we gelled with the locals.

My account would not be complete without paying homage to a marginally downs syndrome lad who played with us in the league at the Station pub. His dad owned and ran a small engineering firm producing pub gambling machines, and I think, pool tables too. He lived in Sudbrooke Park where Lincoln's elite lived. The property had an outside swimming pool and tennis court. He was very canny. He was not good at the tactical side of pool but was a very good single ball potter. He invited me to play tennis with him one summer's day and thrashed the pants off me. Offering me some cans of beer that, no doubt his parents bought, he would remind me of the beers I owed him the next time I saw him in the local as his parents only gave him so much beer money for a night out.

My dear friend was nominated to be the post master general posting the card after each league match. We did well in the first season earning promotion. The committee deemed it necessary to rationalise the leagues and we went up three divisions in one go. We started to lose and even I lost a few games! But suddenly we started to climb the table despite losing. Other teams complained to the secretary that their place in the league did not reflect their wins. It turned out that the card had been doctored and we were somehow winning matches we had lost on the night. My friend was challenged he admitted changing the results before posting the card. We appealed to the secretary and told him of our friend's handicap and said he would be suspended from the team for a month and stripped of his postal duties. They were happy with this and amended the league table accordingly and we were not thrown out of the league or punished in any other way.

Eventually the Station pool team folded and I joined the Nightingale team in Lincoln where a fellow team member and I went on to win the doubles championship, the team won the KO competition and premier division league titles. Other accolades include trialling for England a couple of times but never getting past the first cut. We played against the England side one time and were slaughtered. My mum used to say oh no not another trophy!

Later in life I joined a Kent pool team and the rules had changed dramatically. The governing body had changed the rules in two critical ways to make the game less tactical … At the break, a minimum of four balls have to hit the cushions rather than two previously and after playing a ball either one of the object balls or the white ball or multiples have to hit a minimum of one cushion. My old tactics were out the window and I had to learn the new tactics. In the first season one of our team members was a top player several classes better than me. One night before the match the two of us turned up for some practice frames. On the first I broke and he went on and dished up to whitewash me. I said I know where I went wrong – I broke. The next frame he broke and whitewashed me again. I said I know where I went wrong – I didn't break!

After a break for Covid the league has resumed and my previous form has returned.

9.

My Cars

To distract me from my first degree disappointment my dad and I set out to buy my first car. I bought a Hillman Avenger automatic 1.5 litre on the never never. It was yellow with a black vinyl roof. The colour was of secondary importance to me, the mechanics were more important. The engine was sound and burnt no oil. I equipped it with a stereo cassette player which sat between the front two seats facing backwards with four speakers two at the front and two at the back. I also mounted two fog lights connected to the brake lights which the police confirmed were not too bright. However, I was approached at the traffic lights at the bottom of Lindum hill by a lorry driver telling me they were illegal.

To me it was the business. A friend and colleague at work always drove the twin carb manual geared Avenger and swore by it.

My first run in with the law was one night when my apprentice friend and I parked up outside the liberal club. We had a drink and a game of snooker in the club and then my friend decided to drive to Newark. For some reason I forgot that I had to drive to my village when we got back to Lincoln and I had a few more beers than I should. We had a kebab before setting off home to Lincoln and it was awful, covered in gravy.

When we got back my friend set off ahead of me. Before setting off from home I had filled the carburettor damper with 3 in 1 oil. It was a damp night. The combination of the two meant the car was flying. I could hardly hold her back. I caught up with my friend and overtook him before the traffic lights leading up to Wragby road, went through those lights legally and followed the right hand corner into Wragby road. Arriving at the traffic lights at the Ruskin Avenue turn I stopped at a red light. Looking in the mirror there were the police. They saw that I had seen them and lit up the blue flashing lights. Well that's it I thought, I'm over the drink drive limit and have lost my licence. They duly breathalysed me and I was marginally under. They asked me how much I had had to drink and I conservatively estimated three pints. They let me go, and shaking like a leaf, drove sedately home. Thank goodness for that horrible kebab.

On another occasion I drove to Nottingham to see my LUT hall mate. We were tinkering with my cars engine when he told me to fire it up. I turned the ignition and the starter motor turned and continued to turn. Switch it off my mate said and I dangled the ignition keys in the windscreen with the starter motor still rotating, the solenoid had welded itself on.

We took the car on a holiday round Devon and Cornwall. One night we decided to have a cheap Indian meal out. I chose a Vindaloo not really knowing what to order. The first mouthful was nice, after the second mouthful beads of sweat appeared all over my face. This cheap meal turned out to be anything but. Several pints of lager, an extra portion of rice and a pot of yoghurt later and I still had to leave half of it. Apparently with a hot curry the more you wash the spices off your tongue the hotter the next mouthful is.

My first car a Hillman Avenger automatic 1.5

Then we arrived in Combe Martin. Climbing a steep grassy hill some way above the beach, we were kicking a football to each other. One would kick it up the hill; the other would allow it to roll down and trap it and send it back. Well my mate sold me short and I turned and chased after it. I caught it up a few strides later and was just deciding whether to fall on it with my legs in a figure of 4 and catch it in the formed trap, or run round it and collect it that way. Then I suddenly realised I couldn't stop. This was like the great annual cheese chase down Cooper's hill in Gloucestershire. Out of the corner of my eye I saw a wooden bus shelter and I veered towards it. I shoulder barged it with such force I swear it moved six inches. Two girls with their parents were on the hillside sunbathing and my friend overheard them say "Do you think he's alright?" "He hasn't got up yet". When I got my breath back I made my way back where, at the bottom of the grassy hill, was an 8-foot wide road which would be crossed in two strides leading to an eminently hurdleable fence. Beyond that is a 200 foot drop onto rocks below. I could easily have come to serious harm that day. Even died! I collected the ball and carried it sheepishly up the hill. We walked along the ridge and my friend got sunburnt and so we booked into lodgings for the night rather than camping.

Sheepishly collecting the ball overlooking the precipitous dive over the cliff

View of bay at Coombe Martin from the grassy hill showing just how far I would have fallen if I had have gone over the fence.

The day before on a camp site with the tent

One Friday in February I met my dad at a pub in Nettleham for a few beers before taking home a fish and chip supper to my mum. I had an asthma attack and my inhaler in the car was empty so I set off home post haste. Taking the turn to my home village the steering went light and I lost control crashing into the back of a parked car. Ironically the two elderly passengers were sat in the front seats of the car and it transpired that they had a flat battery. My asthma attack rescinded. They sat there for what seemed an age and eventually I got out of my car to go and speak to them. As soon as I stepped out of the car I nearly fell over on black ice. He went to a nearby phone box to call the police who shortly after came along. My dad turned up and when given permission to go he towed me home. At home I was making a coffee when the policeman turned up at the back door. Instead of putting three teaspoons of sugar and one of coffee in my mug, I put three teaspoons of coffee and one of sugar in – and drank it. He said that a young lad said I was speeding but couldn't take his word for it as he was too young to testify. He said given the black ice it was not surprising I had lost control of the car and no further action would be taken. Ironically we had the bumper off effecting bodywork repairs to the front of the car. More plastic padding required. The radiator was shot so we rang round the scrapyards and found one that had just one serviceable radiator in store. We set off with the old radiator to part exchange it and on arrival in my dad's Marina there was an Avenger with its bonnet up. We came out with the second hand radiator to see the two guys from the Avenger carrying their radiator into the scrapyard. We hastily made our departure. Lessons learnt – ensure ventolins are topped up, don't speed especially on Fridays in February and don't look at the hazard in an emergency but look at the escape route.

My next car was a white Allaggro 1.2 Litre. We part exchanged my Avenger in a private sale. Opening the boot of the Avenger for one final inspection the hinge broke. My dad whipped it off took it to his nearby works and had it welded and replaced it. And so I was the proud owner of a British Leyland Allegro. It was a comfortable ride having hydro gas suspension but lacking in oomph.

Driving to work one Friday in February I was a good three car lengths behind the car in front when it stopped unnaturally fast. I hit the brakes but the gap was still closing fast, my car wasn't stopping so I pressed harder on the brakes. I skidded into the back of the car in front, which was shunted into the car in front of him or so he said. A distant friend got out of the car in front it and I thought it had to be him. When the police came I gave a ridiculously inaccurate estimate of the distance I was driving behind the car in front and was done for driving without due care and attention and fined. I still don't know how that made me a better driver. In truth I was in a skid and needed to take my foot off the brakes and reapply them – cadence braking I was told afterwards. It is worth a note that most modern cars have cadence braking built into the braking system optimised to minimise the stopping distance. By manually lifting your foot off and reapplying the brake pedal you may be duplicating the cadencing resulting in a greater stopping distance. So check if your car has built in cadence braking before physically cadence braking.

In the cars latter days you didn't need to change the oil as it was totally replaced every couple of weeks just by topping it up daily. It didn't let me down driving to Nottingham and back every Friday for my Master's degree, but by the time I traded it in the engine was making a terrible rattling sound. A young lad did the deal and said right lets go for a run in your car. On getting in and starting it up I said it's got a good stereo and duly turned it up as loud as possible. A friend of mine worked as a salesman there and said I had sold them a right lemon that went straight to the scrapyard. I had to agree.

My next two cars were in quick succession were a red Polo and a brown Astra. The Polo pinked on climbing a hill in a high gear due to the petrol needed being 3 star rather than the 2 and 4 star available in the UK. The mechanic said there was nothing wrong having had it up to 100mph on the back roads! The brown 1.2 litre Astra I inherited from my dad. After he died, early the next year I took my mum on holiday to northern Yugoslavia – the Istrian Peninsula. Setting off for the airport I grabbed the passports the ones with the corners not cut off. Arriving at the airport I disabled the car by taking the coil to distributor lead off. On checking in I discovered that I had my dad's old passport instead of mine and they wouldn't let me fly on it. We were an hour early and the flight was delayed by an hour. Apparently the police have been known to do a practice emergency run and fetch the passport but they declined. The only thing for it was to drive home myself and fetch it. I replaced the coil lead and off I went. Needing some petrol I called in at a garage for a splash and dash and put in lead free petrol instead of the usual leaded. Joining the queue to pay a lady in front of me saw I was in a panic and kindly let me queue jump. So off we go again, got 200 yards and the car conked out. I'm in the middle of no-where having wrecked the engine, my mum at the airport, not a member of a breakdown organisation with no mobile phone. The holiday was ruined. I popped the bonnet and the coil lead had come loose. Reconnected it and off I went again. At the Lincoln ring road I saw a policeman holed up on one of the roundabouts and made a mental note for the return journey. Picked up the right passport and set off for the airport. The policeman had gone, so foot down again only to find him parked up on the next roundabout. Negotiating that hazard I set off again. Approaching the Nottingham roundabout I encountered a plain clothes police car and saw the driver subtly radioing in. At the roundabout I didn't indicate right but let him to go straight on then I turned right. Arriving at the airport terminal I parked outside the main doors and went in to see if I had arrived in time. I couldn't find my mum so the helpdesk tannoyed her. They rushed us to the terminal gate and frisked us, I was dangling my car keys telling them to park my car and look after the keys. We ran across the runway apron heading for the plane, luggage in hand just as the baggage handlers were walking away … "no, no put these in the hold" I pleaded. We had made it. The car journey had been the most exciting part of the holiday.

VW polo and the Astra

My next cars were a white Peugeot 205 Gti (1.6) and two Citroen Saxos, a red 16 valve VTS and a silver lesser powerful 8-valve VTR. Exciting times! The Peugeot was very stable and took corners as if on rails. It was so much quicker than I was used to that it took several months before I could reliably use the power. On one occasion my rally driving friends from Ludford were encouraging me to drive faster on the country lanes on the way to a friend's house whose key we had. It was his wedding day. We rounded a corner to find a horse and trap coming the other way. With the aid of the verge we missed them comfortably but the driver of the trap was intent on whipping the car. When we got to my friend's house we apple-pied their bed and rigged a bucket full of water to their loft hatch.

Peugeot 205 1.6 Gti

The Saxo 1.6 16 valve VTS was that much quicker again compared to the Peugeot – 7.8secs from 0-60mph and even more stable in cross winds. The second Saxo I chose as the replacement was the 8-valve version, slower, but it had the old wheel style which I liked so much. Another reason for choosing the VTR was because I was able to replace the skinny spare tyre with a full alloy wheel from the old VTS. These Saxos I have driven for the last 40 years.

My Saxo 1.6 16v VTS and the successor the silver VTR 8v.

10.

Family Sickness

And then my world fell apart. My mum was poorly. They struggled to diagnose what was wrong despite putting cameras down her throat and up her rear end. I swear they would have met in the middle if they had done them both at the same time. They decided to operate on her tummy looking for ulcers but found stomach cancer. They removed all of it having found it early and as the specialist said he re-plumbed her pipework.

My dad looked after her until she was strong enough start to cope but her weight plummeted to less than 4 stone. She couldn't keep food down. Ultimately she lived for two years eating just tinned cream rice. When she had eaten too much she got a pain in her left shoulder. After two years she started eating small meals and had her own tiny dinner plate.

It was all too much for my dad. He didn't think she would pull through and embarked on a downward mental health spiral. He was in and out of mental health wards and hated them. They would give him ECT (Electro Convulsive Therapy) which seemed to reset his memory and for a few hours he was his old self again until his memory of his predicament returned resulting in an overbearing state of self-pity.

It didn't help that he had an inner ear infection which affected his balance and driving ability. Some years earlier he had had a grommet inserted in his inner ear but this only worked for a few months.

I tried for hours to talk through his problems but it was all to no avail. He used to be a good dancer having achieved gold certificate and won a few cups. Music to him was for dancing to but now he started listening to the lyrics which worsened his condition. I tried to tell him that my mum would live but he didn't believe me. She was under weight, describing herself as like having been in Belson concentration camp, but she was a fighter.

I even bought my first bungalow with the notion that he could stay there away from his problems. But my mum would not let him come as he would have been left on his own during the day while I was at work. She was probably right.

Towards the end when I visited him in hospital and took him out for a pint he produced a bottle of tablets which he said he would take all in one go. When we got back to the ward I made him hand them over. What was I to do? If I hadn't done this and he'd have taken them then I never would have forgiven myself. In retrospect having them in his possession was a comfort to him knowing there was always a handy way out.

Then one Sunday night at home he went to bed early and next morning I couldn't rouse him. There was a cocktail of pills scattered on the floor including my mums strong pain killers.

One of the last things he said to me was "I can't laugh". This stayed in my mind for a long time thereafter.

My mum went on to live another 24 years before succumbing ultimately to peritonitis.

Following my dad's death I took my mum on several foreign holidays including a car touring holiday of France, the Istrian peninsula of the then Yugoslavia and Tenerife.

Mum... Mum again...
and Mum and I
on some foreign holidays

11.

Back To Work

11.1. Bulgin

Four years after my dad died there were redundancies in the air at Marconi and this coupled with the family sickness and the reading of John Fowles' *Aristos* may have contributed to my mental illness described in the following chapters. When the first round of redundancies was announced I was one of the unlucky ones. But the HR resources acknowledged my illness and kept me on at a reduced salary which I could afford. A year later and redundancies came around again and this time they let me go. I was not in the right state of mind to work because of the side effects of the anti-psychotic drugs I was on. I did briefly get taken on as a burglar alarm technician with a neighbour but had to give it up as I was still not well enough to work.

Two years after being made redundant I got a job at Bulgin – a power supply manufacturer, as a one man department for the repair of field faulty switched mode and linear power supplies. I had to book in the daily arrivals on a bespoke data base, fix the faults, test the PSU's and organise their despatch.

This lasted just under two years and it was the worst paid job I had ever had and the management worked me the hardest. Every couple of weeks I would get a reminder that I was working on mains driven circuits by getting an electric shock. One of the Bulgin family members would come to see our managing director in his TVR sports car, not to say that I was jealous as I had my 205 Gti.

I was grateful that I had held a job down again after my illness.

11.2. Ericsson

Within a month of being made redundant from Bulgin I secured a contractors job with Ericsson in Scunthorpe making racks of equipment for the purpose of transmitting data to wide area pagers. I loved it – best job ever. I was immediately paid 50% more than Bulgin with more small increases to come. Initially I got on well with all the staff but as my skills showed, a rift developed between me and a technician on the team. When the rack was all but finished I had to connect a powerful battery at the foot of the rack and my friendly technician would regularly jump on a large bubble wrap cell from the packing cartons sounding a huge bang, which frightened the life out of me. In all the racks that we built I never wired the battery up backwards.

Nearing the end of the contract I saw a job advertised at Worksop, still Ericsson but repairing production faulty mobile phones. I left Ericsson at Scunthorpe before the full consignment of equipment was shipped and I was told my successor actually did connect the battery backwards. Unsure what the outcome was, maybe overheating of the wires to melting point?

The guys at Worksop were very mischievous. If they found you alone in the toilets, especially in the cubicles, they would ping the lights out leaving you in pitch black to finish up and fumble your way out. It was worse when you were caught in the urinals. Once they pinged the foreman.

Whilst there, the management set up Saint Circles which

were essentially quality circles. Groups of individuals set up to make improvements and money saving ideas. I was asked to run a team of fault finders. We were named the Woodworkers. We were successful enough to send one of us on a business trip to Virginia USA and I was the lucky one to be voted to go. Whilst there, I met a lady who would become a lifelong friend. So happy was I on meeting her that back at the hotel after a few mandatory scoops of Drambuie at the bar I set off to my room. On arriving at my floor I sprinted down the long corridor toward my room. I had learned recently to float when running which meant increasing the stride and bouncing higher, thus "floating", and running faster. On reaching top speed I elongated my stride. Unfortunately the corridor sloped downward and my lead leg failed to contact the ground. I fell, chest first. Winded and grazed, I lay there for 5 minutes, gingerly got up and went to my room. Many years later her husband died and after a suitable time, I proposed to her over the internet. But when push came to shove I couldn't leave Blighty. She went on to marry a guy with the same surname as me and the initials JC. Ironic I thought.

There were several of us from Lincoln working at Worksop and we used to lift share. My dad never liked car sharing but I enjoyed the company along with the money saving on car expenses. I later heard that Bulgin had folded and a couple of my colleagues there got jobs at Ericsson Worksop.

Always keen to participate in company share schemes I had the opportunity to borrow £11,000 and invest in a company debenture scheme. For a couple of years the price of Ericsson shares gradually increased to the break-even price and then technology related shares soared and there were days when my investment would rise £1000 or more in a day. It was a time limited investment and I should have cashed in when they were worth £30000 in profit but I hung on. Then the stock market crash of 1986 occurred and I watched my investment dive back below the profit threshold price again. A valuable lesson learnt. When the contract matured I just let it run out and the monies I had borrowed were paid back to the bank so all I lost were the interest payments on the borrowed money which were covered by another share scheme I had with Ericsson.

Dabbling in the stock market is for the long haul. By the time an individual finds out about short term company news that affects the share price the value has invariably already moved.

Four years on and Ericsson closed. This was despite the loyal workforce adopting round the clock 12 hour shifts. Orbitel, as it was before it was bought out by Ericsson. Orbitel was one of the first companies to make mobile phones – the original "brick" phones famously used in the City.

11.3. British Aerospace

During the notice period at Ericsson I secured at interview at BAe. Driving back from the first interview at Rochester the head gasket on my Saxo VTS blew. I tried limping home but had to yield at the next lay-by. Fortunately I was in the RAC by now and many hours later they delivered me and my car from near Cambridge to a garage in Nettleham. Many thanks go to the RAC. Many pounds later with a new catalytic convertor and head gasket and skimmed cylinder head, I went for the second interview with the manager who was unavailable the first time round.

I got the job. Design for test engineer, with a 30% increase in pay. It took me a year to find a bungalow suitable for my mother and I and it was just affordable with a maximum call on my mortgage eligibility. I wouldn't say I pulled up any trees but my manager seemed happy with my work and I earned a pay rise on each of the 10 years I worked there. I did develop an excel spread sheet to assess test effectiveness. The best test philosophy was boundary scan – a method of designed in connectivity.

I was seconded to help with the upgrade of computers. This entailed the replacement of all computers on site outside of normal working hours. This assignment earned a silver chairman's award for the team at the company's awards dinner dance.

Another assignment was to repatriate some test equipment from Edinburgh.

Later I maintained and researched an excel spread sheet, a data base of component suitability for RoHS – Restriction of Hazardous Substances and in particular their lead free status.

My mum died in hospital of peritonitis just before my 50th birthday which was partly due to the consequence of her stomach cancer operation 25 years or so earlier. When finally admitted to hospital the doctors said they could operate to clean out her abdomen of faeces that they believed caused the peritonitis but that she would have only a 50% chance of surviving. My mum was adamant she didn't want any further surgery and the doctors said after she died that her chances of survival were actually less than 10%.

If only my dad had believed in me that she would live on after her cancer scare he could have had another 24 years with her.

Ten years after joining the company, redundancy raised its ugly head again.

11.4. Smallholders club

Aged 63 I was taken on as doorman at the Smallholders club, a members' social club, within walking distance of my home, to cover for a regular doorman having a minor operation. This resulted in my covering for absence, sickness and holidays on a zero hours' basis.

With Xmas looming the Steward was short of staff behind the bar so I was conscripted on an as needed basis. The cash was useful as low interest rates meant my savings capital was reducing.

I have recently been trained to perform cellar duties but I struggle to lift full barrels of beer to install them on their plinths due to my small arms and dodgy back. It remains to be seen if I cover for the steward's holiday.

I have recently been promoted to glass collection and loading and unloading the dish washer and restacking the glasses' shelves.

12.

Retirement

At the age of 52 I took early retirement. I did apply for a few jobs locally but was not successful. I was disappointed with how few electronics' companies there were in Kent. There were more in Lincolnshire before they all closed down.

My mum had left me with enough money not to have to work and I did not want to leave the locality as everything I needed was at hand – shops, pubs, takeaways, Indian restaurants, and most importantly a social club. In the club I formed a good social circle making friends with neighbours and regulars. There is a snooker table upstairs. Snooker is a passion of mine although it is far too skilled for my limited ability. None the less I still like it. A group of 5 of us formed a curry club frequenting the many Indian restaurants in the Medway region once a month. This has now increased to once a week for me, my neighbour and good friend.

Never keen on cooking in my early days as I didn't like heat on my hands, I have become quite a proficient cook, good enough to feed myself. It's amazing what you can do with hot chilli powder. If it doesn't clear your sinuses then there's not enough spice in the dish. Even gravy benefits from a desert spoon of hot chilli powder. If it gives you the trots next day then it's too spicy. When my mum was alive no spices were allowed as she couldn't stomach them. She was a good plain food cook and used to make stews, which, when she had taken her portion, I used to spice up the remainder. I also got my spice fix from takeaways. Her Sunday lunches were legendary which I miss greatly.

I also enjoy reading with favourite authors being Tom Sharpe, Alistair Maclean and latterly Bernard Cornwell. My thanks go to a friend that gave me the Sharpe novels which, contrary to my pacifism, make good reading and give an insight into the bravery of soldiers in the peninsular wars of the 1800s.

I enjoy music of many genres from the rock music of Roy Orbison, Buddy Holly, Bryan Adams and Fleetwood Mac to classical music including Bach, Beethoven, Mozart and Rachmaninov.

Section 2
Spiritual Awakening

1.

In The Beginning

Aged 32 I had a persistent thought that I was Jesus following the reading of a philosophical book called the Aristos by John Fowles. The age is particularly relevant as this was the same age Jesus began his calling. How could this notion be true I wondered? If I had the same DNA as Jesus then this could be a possible explanation. In Revelations 3:12 and 19:12 it states that Jesus would return with a new name. The new name infers a new person by way of different nature and nurture. You cannot reincarnate the old incarnation. This is consistent with the hypothesis of reincarnation. I am now happy to be me in the 21st Century as a different person to the original incarnation particularly because of modern education and life events.

I have undertaken to provide a sample of saliva to have my DNA analysed for my origins. The results are in and it confirms that I am 53% Welsh, 40% English and North-western European (primarily West Yorkshire), 4% Swedish and Danish and 3% Scottish. This confirms my parentage so no immaculate conception for me. It does say that the analysis only goes back to 1700s though. I was hoping for a link to the Middle East, and Nazareth especially, for obvious reasons. However I do still believe I am the Messiah. It does say in the Ancestry DNA blurb that the further back in time you go the more diluted the DNA markers are, so I may yet have Jesus' DNA. Had I been one of Jesus' disciples I would have relocated Jesus away from Jerusalem and the Romans as soon as possible after his purported resurrection. What better place to go than England and indeed Lincolnshire, my birthplace. It would be another 56 to 68 or more years before the Romans would arrive to found Lincoln itself. They say that the phoenix rises from its ashes? Interestingly there is a Jerusalem in Lincolnshire, a small village not too far from Lincoln.

Another quote in Revelations 19:12 says that no man knew but he himself … that he was the new name. This appears to be true as I have not yet had any human accept my ideas or acknowledge my claim to be the Messiah. I have had confirmation from a disembodied voice as described in the chapter Scottish Business Trip. I have had many people say the theories are interesting. I leave it to you to make up your own mind. Judge me on my ideas. For me to be accepted as the Messiah in the Jewish faith I have to be a Jew, which plainly I am not. I was born with a retracted foreskin to the extent that I am hypospadic. I don't know if this qualifies me to be Jewish or not. Probably not. Maybe I have been reborn a gentile to broaden inclusion in the new religion?

There have been many males in the past that have claimed this identity and I dare say there will be in the future too. May be the high that we experience was the same that JC had all those years ago?

If not accepted this story may help other aspirants.

The links are tenuous. In truth I cannot identify hard evidence to support my claim. It is a belief.

The following chapters detail the experiences I had when high on oxytocin. If the paranormal exists then it is when high on oxytocin. Of course all of the following events may be ascribed to coincidence.

2.

Lightning

Early on in my quest a storm was brewing in the distance. I felt the urge to converse with it. I thought of a question and waited affirmation by way of a lightning strike.

As the conversation progressed the storm was closing in. Originally I was walking around my front garden but felt the urge to take it to my local pub. There I looked out of the front window onto a field and continued the conversation.

The storm grew closer and closer and it seemed that it was homing in on me. There may be some scientific merit in this as on the website 'how things work' it describes how objects emit streamers of oppositely charged particles which lightning locks onto. So maybe in the high state of mind I was emitting a huge streamer that the storm was homing in on.

As the lightning came overhead I adopted a crucifix style stance and thought or said if you would have me receive the power then so be it, but quickly thought no – absolute power corrupts absolutely.

As I turned to walk away in rejection of the power I thought it has to go somewhere. So I thought give it to the church thinking of the small village church nearby.

Suddenly there was a flash of lightning and simultaneously a thunder clap meaning the storm was directly overhead, the lights in the pub went out and the folk at the bar dived for cover.

Next day in the local Lincolnshire Echo newspaper was the appended photograph of Lincoln Cathedral purportedly being hit by three lightning strikes. On closer inspection the left hand strike is just missing the Cathedral and I believe the other strikes grounded in the fields behind the Cathedral. But it is the symbolism that matters.

Lightning strikes "hitting" Lincoln Cathedral

Who wields a trident if not the Devil? So was I tempted by the devil and turned him down as Jesus did in the wilderness? Certainly, if the lightning had have hit me it would have been the end for me. I don't actually believe in the devil so maybe it was a test from God? Or just coincidence?

I have never communed with storms before or since.

3.

The Psyche Handshake

My dad taught me to return a handshake grip commensurate with the grip offered. Hence if a person has a light grip you do not exceed theirs. He said this would keep me safe but did not elucidate how.

Since going high this has taken on new meaning to me. A lighter grip to mine suggests that the person is more spiritual, or has the potential to be more spiritual, than I. That is assuming the person is exerting their full grip strength. They may not be returning their full capability because they are physically infirm, are too strong for the majority of their kinfolk and have no wish to injure their counterpart or just because they have no desire to enter the contest and offer a limp handshake. Also persons not yet fully grown up give an erroneous indication.

A more powerful grip than mine quantifies them as being an Earthly person. My thought is that the more physically strong you are the more likely it is that oxytocin is suppressed.

In the psyche handshake, both parties increase their grip strength until one or the other cannot match the grip strength of the counterpart. At this point the less strong party involuntarily totally releases their grip to nothing, which should be sensed by the stronger party, at which point the handshake is over. If the stronger party continues to increase their grip then this will result in pain to the hand of the weaker party.

I have known some Earthly people to perform the psyche handshake and on release reaffirm the grip suggesting that they are asserting that they had greater grip to give.

Chapters entitled the three Welshmen and the Welsh wedding are also relevant as these were examples of the handshake strengths along with the model of humanity which defines spirituality and Earthliness.

Other very strongly gripped people have come close to breaking bones in my hand, such was their strength.

I also wonder if people with stronger grips have lower thresholds of pain than their spiritual counterparts. This may make an interesting project for a Psychology student.

A controlled handshake may also signify mental control too.

The term handshake refers to a person exerting their maximum limit of strength whereupon they start to shake with effort. Those of us that have struggled opening a jar will be familiar with this concept. When you get two people that are evenly matched in terms of grip strength and they both shake with effort then this is the maximum hand-shake. You do not physically move the handshake up and down.

Women's handshakes compared to a man's are generally weaker so does this mean that they are more spiritual than their male counterparts? Certainly they are more emotional and probably more loving than males.

It is worth mentioning that my wrists and arms are particularly thin giving rise to my being termed as being gentle as a lamb.

4.

Newport Arch

Making my way home early one afternoon I saw a work colleague and good friend walking in the city and stopped the car to greet him and asked if he would like to discuss some of my ideas. So we drove to the Bailgate area of Lincoln and parked facing Newport Arch. During the conversation a Norman arch appeared in the sky perfectly framed above the real Roman arch. After a few ponderous moments we realised it was the vapour trails from the Red Arrows display team practising over the fields near Nettleham.

A little while later the car behind us rolled driverless into the back of my car. A shopkeeper across the road saw what had happened and directed me to the errant car owner's house. He came out explaining that the cars handbrake was faulty. I advised him to park his car with the front wheels turned into the curb.

Events like this only seem to occur when I am high. The heightened senses when high on oxytocin make these events more noticeable. Maybe they do happen all the time but just go unnoticed. Maybe they are these just coincidences or they the paranormal existing whilst in this high state of mind.

5.

Driving Anecdotes

Setting off to work in Worksop at 5am in the morning from my home near Lincoln on a cold and frosty morning I pulled up at the junction in the neighbouring village of Scothern in my Peugeot 205 Gti (1.6l) when an old jalopy pulled in front of me doing about 20mph and it took the country lane I needed to cross the countryside on single track roads to get to the main road to Worksop. Now I had never seen this car before or after except for this one day when there was black ice on the back roads. To this day I believe he was sent to keep me safe. We cautiously drove this back lane until at the next junction we both turned right but he carried on straight whereas I took another left down another country lane at a very modest pace then onto gritted main roads to my destination.

On another occasion my control in driving was tested whilst high. I was travelling down Tritton road in Lincoln when Bryan Adams' everything I do I do for you came on the radio. A particular favourite of mine at the time and I went higher and higher but my foot on the accelerator remained locked without recourse to going faster. The tendency when your brain is working faster because of the oxytocin rush is to drive faster and more dangerously, but I was able to retain control.

6.

The Three Welshmen

Three Welshmen came into my local pub and challenged me to a game of pool. I am quite an accomplished player particularly good at the tactical side of the game. I beat the most Earthly player quite easily, the Carer, I beat quite comfortably too. In the model of humanity the people at the higher end of the diagram are the Spirituals those at the lower end are the Earthlies and the people bordering the axis are the Carers. I don't recall if I played the most spiritual Welshman that night.

Two of the three returned the following night the most Earthly being missing. The most spiritual was quite confrontational, spoiling for a fight. We locked horns over a game of pool. After a little tactical manoeuvring I attacked only to snooker myself on my last ball. Determined not to be beaten I wound myself up to play an almost impossible masse shot with fade to running side. I was psyching myself up when the Welshman trashed the game as he didn't want to see me pull off an almost impossible shot.

Now he was really pitting for a fight. I offered him a handshake and he took it with intent but I was right in that he was more spiritual than I and I held his grip. My judgement was correct. We released the handshake and I took my leave. I never saw them again.

7.

Bipolar Or Not? My Self-diagnosis

Before I enter into this chapter I would like to affirm that I have never taken illicit drugs and that the high I experienced was perfectly natural. I believe the drugs generated by my body were that associated with spiritual love – oxytocin. Also I have never hallucinated or heard voices in my head.

The heightened mental state of love is very desirable. Paul Merson spoke of the addiction of gambling and had an MRI (Magnetic Resonance Image) brain scan where he was shown pictures of family and food with no appreciable increase in brain activity. However when shown pictures of roulette and cards his brain really lit up with activity. I believe the same increased brain activity is true of love. For me it was one of the happiest times of my life, I was thinking faster and crosswords became easier. An example of higher perception was when I was driving to a job interview down south when, on a busy motorway, indicating to go into the outside lane I detected the oncoming headlight dip down indicating that he was braking to let me out. Your taste buds are more receptive as experienced when I partook of a particular pint of bitter, on changing to another brand the taste buds on my tongue burned. A further side effect of love is uncontrolled spending of money. The only example of this with me was buying 30 copies of John Fowles' *Aristos*. When I came to my senses the shop took half back and I had no trouble in giving the others away. Maybe this is why Jesus said you can't serve Mammon (worldly possessions) and God?

Before I had developed the model of humanity which is the basis of a new religion the only way I could think of inducing the kingdom of heaven was to push my high to the extreme and see what happened. As in the song by Sweet, love is like oxygen you get too much you get too high … not enough and you're gonna die. Don't know about the you're gonna die element as countless people live without experiencing love as highlighted when Prince Charles was asked on camera if he was in love with princess Diana and he famously said "whatever love is".

Although diagnosed as bipolar the only low I experience is immediately after a massive high when once again I had failed to bring about the kingdom of heaven.

In the first instance I went to see my GP at his home with a notion that laughter was the cure for mental illness derived from my dad saying he could not laugh when consumed with depression. So, armed with a laughter box, I asked to go to a mental ward. Needless to say I was admitted to the ward and the laughter box confiscated. That night the patients and I watched a particularly funny episode of last of the summer wine and the mood in the ward was lifted.

I felt safe enough in the ward to push higher to see where it led me with the aim of bringing about the kingdom of heaven with a massive psychic surge not knowing what it was or how to achieve it. The high is very pleasurable, one feels invincible. I was diagnosed as bipolar despite not experiencing depression.

I believe to this day that the high is spiritual love. What is love? Love is the drug which Brian Ferry sang about many years ago. That drug has now been confirmed as oxytocin.

Having pushed myself higher than could be controlled, I hit fight or flight mode. Symptoms of which are temporary cold hands and cold feet. The cold hands/feet are physiologically due to the body constricting blood vessels in the limbs to prevent excess blood loss in the event of injury.

Other side effects of being high include requiring less sleep, endless energy and reduced appetite and as previously mentioned can involve reckless spending of money. As Robert Palmer sang about love – can't eat, can't sleep there's no doubt you're in deep.

When high thoughts and ideas come thick and fast but before you can explain them you have forgotten what you had thought up.

Another perception when high is that you think that the media is specifically broadcasting to you be it songs, jollity or TV programs that you need for information purposes. One book in particular for me was the Aristos by John Fowles. It outlined my philosophy on life to a tee – except for death. I believe death is a finality. That is until your DNA is replicated either by natural conception and birth or in years to come by manufactured methods which, incidentally, is how I believe people will be brought back from the dead. Albeit to go through the growing up process all over again – Reincarnation. As we all have a unique DNA then replication of this life force results in rebirth. Albeit the new birth will develop a new and different person due to different nature and nurture. You cannot be reborn as the old incarnation. Reference Revelations 20:13 which says Jesus will re-emerge with a new name. Death is final. There is no afterlife. Also without a functional brain and indeed a complete cessation of the thought processes as in dementia and Alzheimer's a person's memory and thought processes are lost.

During this heightened phase I was confronted by some nurses. I was in the fight or flight state of mind and being a pacifist the only option was to run. I ran out of the ward down the stairs to the main entrance, closely followed by the baying pack, Confronted with closed doors to the outside I reasoned that the doors must open outwards as, if there was an emergency, a throng of people would push up against the doors and it would be impossible to open the doors inwards. So I ran full tilt at the doors and they didn't budge resulting in a nasty bump on my forehead. The nurses caught up with me and carried me to my room where they removed my trousers and underwear. In my mind I would have been a good 'ride' for a homosexual even though I am heterosexual through and through. They injected me in the posterior with a sedative in my mind to pacify me enough to penetrate me but which knocked me out completely.

Next day I felt well until they medicated me because of the side effects of the drugs causing endless restless legs due to the interference of the drugs on my central nervous system.

Another important point is that I have been able to control and limit the high as described in Chapter 11 *The Scottish Business Trip* and avoided going over the top. So there is no need for medication. I look forward to coming off the medication once this book is published and return to my rightful place in the kingdom of heaven using the medication as necessary to avoid going too high but only if absolutely necessary. I intend practising meditation to control my brain. Having redefined the kingdom of heaven in the next section I no longer have the need to push the oxytocin levels in my blood uncontrollably high in order to invoke the kingdom of heaven through psychic energy. As I now believe that psychic energy is a myth. Any potential followers of my theories will expect me to be able to control myself without medication whilst in the heavenly state of mind. I do not recommend those of you who are on medication to cease taking it without the support of the health system.

Many people with mental illness are ground breakers in their fields of expertise. To name a few:

Vincent Van Gogh – Painting

Brian Wilson – Music

Stephen Fry – Comedy

Spike Milligan – Comedy

Me – Religion and peoples

My apologies go to the many of you of whom I have not mentioned.

Brian Wilson once said the higher the high, the lower the low meaning depression. In my case I believe I am at the border of Spirituality/Earthliness and so my extremities are not too high as to experience the lows.

Following reports that they have identified oxytocin as the love hormone with the objective of applying a nasal spray to reduce the appetite of over-weight and obese people with a view to reducing their weight. One of the side effects of being in love is reduced appetite as identified in the song addicted to love by Robert Palmer. The hormone is generated by the hippocampus when the neurons are stimulated therein and the hormone is released into the bloodstream by the posterior pituitary gland. This,

I am sure, is what happened to me. The next time I go high I will ask for a blood test to detect if oxytocin is in my blood. Some bipolar patients may subconsciously be invoking depression in order to suppress mania?

In the sermon-on-the mount one of the categories for entry into the kingdom of heaven is those individuals who are poor of spirit or in today's parlance the mentally ill. I re-emphasise I do not yet recommend your coming off your medication; this has to be done with medical blessing. I do that which I intend to at my own risk in the knowledge that I have the back-up of Olanzapine.

The discovery of oxytocin will enable everyone to experience love and experience the kingdom of heaven if they so wish.

I encourage the medical profession to see if oxytocin has curative powers over serious brain conditions.

8.

Shadow Boxing

On one occasion when hospitalised I was venting my frustrations by shadow boxing a full length curtain when another prospective Jesus came along and saw me.

When I came back from a weekend's leave this other prospective Jesus had picked a fight with another inmate and had come off second best having been badly beaten. I recall the nurse talking to the victor who said he was glad not to have been the recipient of the onslaught as he would not have been allowed to defend himself, being a British NHS carer.

I remember thinking this prospective Jesus had failed his audition for the post. I feel all I have been through so far has been a test of suitability to be the Messiah.

9.

Early Drug Side Effects

Having been diagnosed with bipolar I was first treated with Lithium. This only works in a small window of dosage which requires regular blood tests to confirm acceptable levels. I didn't like being on Lithium.

Next came Mellerill which made me quite unwell. Restless legs because of interference with my central nervous system. Also when discharged from hospital I went for some petrol and couldn't sign my name on the invoice slip. I had to literally think to my hand up, down, left or right. Fortunately a second drug Kemedrin counteracted the side effects of the primary drug.

More recently I have been treated with Amisulperide and now Olanzapine which stop me from going high. I do look forward to the time when I return to my enhanced state of mind.

10.

The Welsh Wedding

Invited to the homeland of my mother in Nov 2000 we arrived at the host's house in good time. That night the host and I went for a drink at the local club. Being keen on pool I left him with his friends to watch the local players. When last orders were called I went to empty my bladder only to find on returning to the bar the host had departed. I ran after him where upon he said 'go your own way', so I ran on ahead to circle round the block and come the long way round to his house.

Being concerned for my welfare as I was acting out of character, as thought by my uncle, my mum called for an ambulance. Initially they were more concerned for the host as he had run after me and suffered chest pains .They eventually took me to A&E. An Asian doctor assessed me. He got off his chair to crouch below me whereupon I determined to get lower than he in respect of his authority. He had me wait for an ambulance to take me to a psychiatric ward.

In the meantime the doctor went to a side room to perform a minor operation on a fellow nurse's arm. I cleaned a little rubbish from under a desk getting approval to dispose of an item I was unsure of. Then I crept to the doorway where the doctor was performing surgery. Chased off by the matron, I crept back to watch further.

Eventually the ambulance arrived and took me away for what seemed a very long journey away from Llanelli.

During the journey I feigned an anxiety attack and later actually felt anxious about the distance they were taking me.

Arriving at Carmarthen hospital I was shown to a ward where there was no sleeping privacy and determined to stop up all night.

Next morning I met a patient who was readmitted for taking illicit drugs. I suggested he cut the drugs weaker and he seemed stunned at this obvious advice.

My turn came to see the doctor "I shouldn't be here" I kept saying. Eventually he convinced me that ranting wasn't helping and they agreed to discharge me without medicating me, on condition that I take a Zopiclone sleeping tablet when I got back to the hotel.

The druggie was astounded that I had been released on such terms and held my hand as we walked out of the hospital telling me to stay grounded – not to show signs of being high.

I walked to the train station and caught the next train to Llanelli. I remember the countryside being very pretty but was too tired to fully take it all in.

Arriving at Llanelli I walked to the hotel we were staying at, which was a minor marathon in itself. This was the same venue that the wedding reception was being held at. As agreed I slept for a few hours.

Initially the host didn't want me at the wedding at which my mum wanted us to go home there and then, however the host relented and we sat at the back of the church for the ceremony. When the host accompanied the bride into the church he seemed pleased to see us there.

At the reception my mum's sister was upset that my mum had the only picture of their parents. I quelled the argument by promising I would use my uncle's computer and peripherals to copy the photograph and other relevant photos to generate copies and send them to all my mum's family. An onlooker was heard to say that he (– me) handled that situation well.

Later that night I met a guy and we invented a game of transferring an almost empty cigarette packet from the back of one of our hands to the back of other. He was too Earthly and insensitive to control the frictional transfer. I took control and had enough sensitivity to accomplish the task.

Later, after dancing for many an hour, I leant against the wall at the disco and it opened and I went through to an unused restaurant. Rather than walking through walls the divider was a hanging suspended partition.

Late on, I sat with cigarette packet man along with an Earthly guy and his wife. I determined to teach him the psyche handshake but every time I reached the limit of my grip strength he was unable to detect the point of my grip release and continued on to crush my hand. I asked cigarette packet man if he understood what I was trying to do and he said I was trying to teach love. Eventually I had to admit defeat as my hand hurt too much to continue.

So maybe the psyche handshake is not for everyone. In retrospect I would try to teach it differently to avoid injury – particularly to me! I would describe the gradual increase in grip strength and the sensitivity necessary to detect the weaker person's sudden and total release of grip. Then, and only then, would I demonstrate it by asking the person not to return grip and show the point at which I would release to see if the adversary would feel the difference.

We were joined at about 3am by a team of paramedics who had come for a rest break.

We moved onto a game I had played at school which

I taught to the children at the function. It comprised drawing a race track on a blank piece of paper. Included were chicanes, where the road narrows, and bends and curves. The first racing driver would then balance a long pencil on its point with one finger on the top of the pencil. You would begin with the sharp pointed end of the pencil on the start grid. Then by slowly slanting the pencil until it flicked a line on the paper race track, resulting in the pencil flying away. Where the pencil mark cut the track or, if it was totally within the boundaries of the track, where the pencil line faded to nothing would be where the next flick would be taken from at their next turn. Then the next racing driver would have a turn. First round the track wins. I determined to teach the muscle man's wife but she said she knew how to do it so I let her have her way. When she finished I showed her what the 12-year-olds had done. Compared to the kids' effort hers looked like the 6-year -olds' effort.

At that point I made my excuses and left for bed.

Next day my cousin's husband drove my mum and me around the local area looking for suitable properties for my mum to return to her roots but the neighbourhood looked run down and she eventually decided to come with me to Kent.

11.

The Scottish Business Trip

Working latterly for Ericsson they had announced the closure of both sites in Carton in Lindrick near Worksop and two engineers, myself and my boss were sanctioned to recover some test equipment racks from Glasgow.

I was quite high at the time having had an episode at work just the day before, but they allowed me to accompany them. Two vans were used, my boss and I in one, the other two engineers in the other van.

On the way up, we stayed at Coatbridge, a hotel by a lake, as I remember.

Playing a joke on my compatriots I dressed for evening dinner in a garish silver shirt, gaudy shorts, knee high tartan socks and trainers and went to meet the guys in the foyer. The two engineers were there and without saying anything they just looked at each other with incredulity. What? Said I, oh I've forgotten the tie. Whereby I went back to my room and redressed much more conservatively.

Coming back from Glasgow I knew I would not sleep that night because I was high. So I sat in the foyer listening to music. Late on there was some classical music that was very soft with increasingly longer bouts of silence. I believe it was the theme music to the Mummy films but I have never confirmed this. The music had the effect of sensitising me as I listened ever more intently for the ever softening music.

Suddenly there was an upbeat melody that had me

dancing in my chair the like of which I had not heard before. It instantly propelled me higher and higher until I had to say no more and refused point blank to go beyond my capability.

A male voice replaced the music on the speaker system, 'Do you know who I am?' it said. 'No' said I. 'I know who you are', the voice went on 'You are Jesus'. I thanked the voice and The Who's *Magic Bus* came over the speaker system and breakfast commenced.

So who was this mystical voice if not God himself? For many a year I have craved confirmation of my previous identity from a human. Was this the time that I had passed the audition?

Driving home with my boss, he had me ring my allotted psychiatric nurse back in Lincoln who urged me take medication. I had brought some with me but it was in my overnight bag in the other van. We rang them and arranged to meet at the harbour in Dunbar.

I went to buy a drink to wash the tablets down and an ice cream. The seagulls watched me eat my treat with envious eyes, when I got to the cone I crushed it and threw it to the sea gulls. They consumed it with loud cries of appreciation.

Resuming the journey I could feel the tablets working and bringing me down from the high, much to my boss's relief.

Section 3
Theories

1.

The Humanitarian Model And Theory

I am defining the Kingdom of Heaven as a living entity; it is a state of mind brought about by the generation of oxytocin and is not a place where dead people go to be in paradise with God. Previously what was heaven for one person was hell to another. My interpretation of being in heaven is a state of mind brought about by oxytocin.

I do not claim that this will cure all the ailments of humanity but it is the basis of a religion where the basic belief is quantifying that some people experience love through internal generation of oxytocin and the balance of populous do not. It may be that the majority of women populate the love quadrant of the diagram and the men the earthly domain.

The origin of this model is a quote from the bible – Matthew 11:11 in which it is said that the least in the Kingdom of Heaven (KoH) is greater than John the Baptist (JtB).

Revelations implores churches to take heed – *"To him that hath an ear let him hear what the spirit saith unto the churches"* It is not said once but many times over … Revelations 2:7, 2:11, 2:17, 2:29, 3:6, 3:13 and 3:22. This implies that the churches have got it wrong and that the incumbent has something new to say, which I have.

The model is built in stages so the reader can see its evolution.

Diagrammatically:

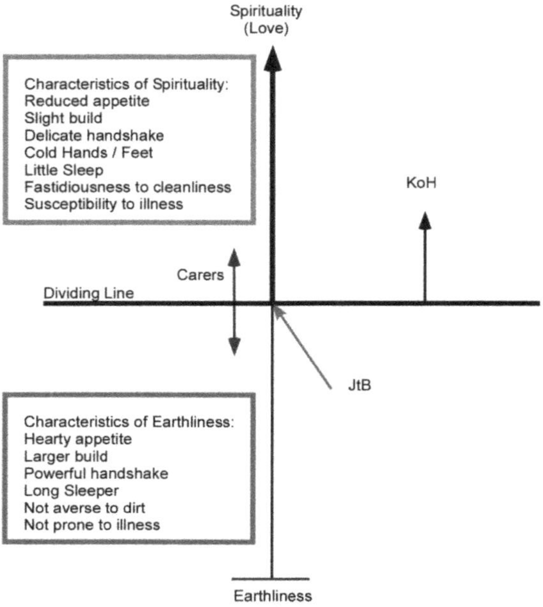

I believe the carers of society sit either side of the dividing line.

Now where on this diagram would you put Jesus (JC)? My local vicar said way off the spirituality scale.

But I assert that he was just on the spiritual scale. Why? Firstly, because he was able to associate with the common man. A highly spiritual man currently lives isolated in a monastery on a mountain. Secondly it is quoted that he is the first and the last … the first if you are looking upwards from the dividing line and last when viewed down from above. It is quoted many times in Revelations – 1:11, 1:17 and 2:8 to quote just a few.

The churches are expecting some supernatural being whereas in reality Jesus and his reincarnate are one in the same, the average man.This is why he will go undetected until his hair turns white as snow as stated in Revelations 1:14.

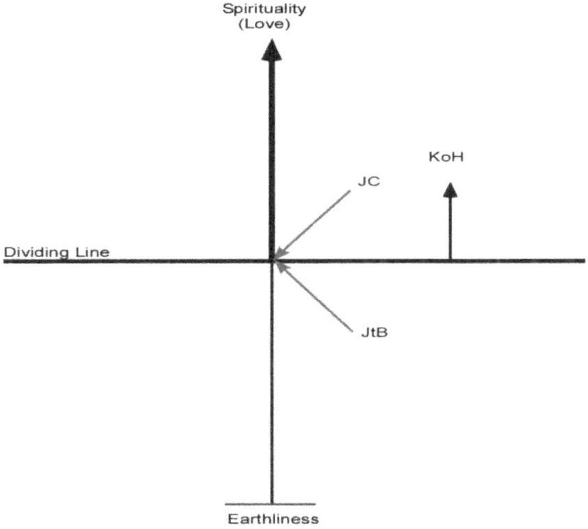

Now, the whole of humanity fits on these scales as either earthly or spiritual. I assert that this is the new heaven and earth referred to in Revelations 21:1. It is not in my remit to assign a place for each of you but is up to you to assess, except that as the gatekeeper, my personal psyche handshake determines spiritualism or earthliness and the approximate degree of either.

A close friend of mine asserted that you are not pigeon holed to one point on the chart but move up and down. This is intuitively correct as you fall in and out of love and consequently in and out of the k-o-h and in my case medically treated to keep me in the Earthly domain.

However I am resistant to this as it becomes too much like a mood plot. So I assert that your position on the chart is your quiescent point – a balance point from which you move up and down according to the chemical content that is love in your brain. That drug has now been identified as Oxytocin.

The purpose of defining characters is intended for all members of society to accept each other without prejudice.

In terms of the cars we drive:

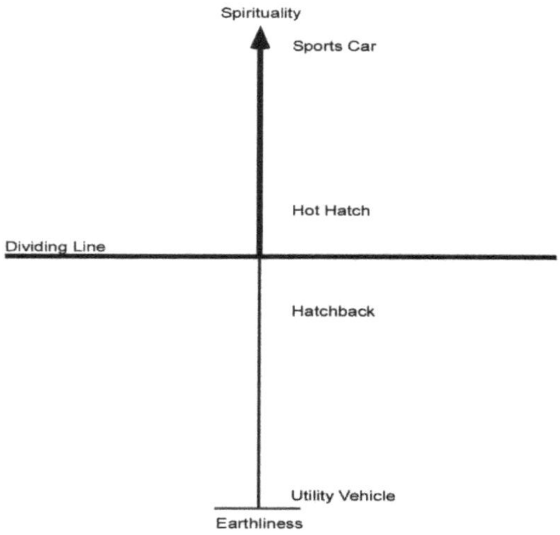

Obviously dependent upon affordability and practicality of purpose!

This is by no means definitive and you are free to choose the car of your choice.

In terms of horses:

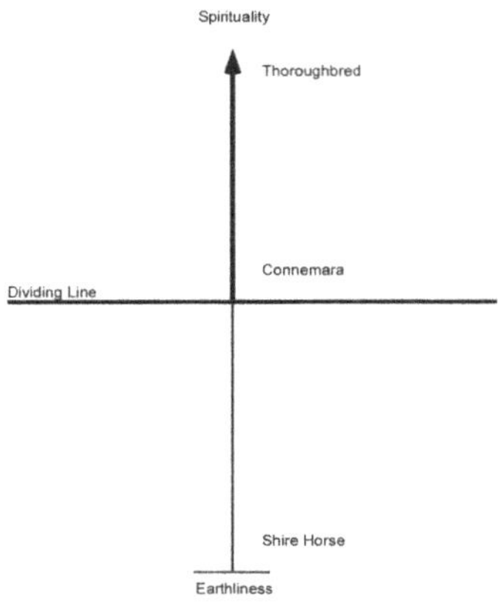

The classic diagram for assessment of mood is the high/ depressive chart.

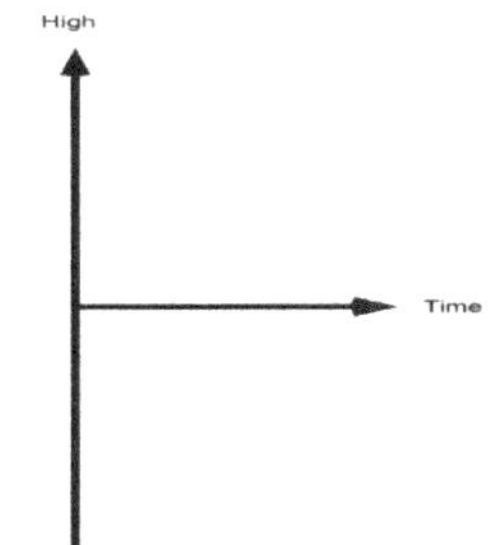

The high and low axis is graded in divisions of 1 to 10 and the time by days. The mood of the individual is then plotted according to their sense of elation or depression. This is different from my model.

Alternatively one might introduce a y axis of higher and lower:

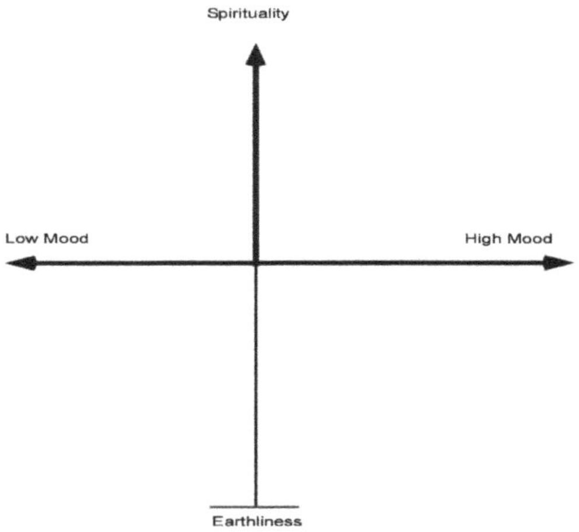

One might add a z-axis entitled time to give a mood plot independent of oxytocin levels. This assumes that your oxytocin level is not responsible for the high. The advantage of this is that if your oxytocin level is constant it gives you a discrete place in the K-o-H. Personally I favour the moving in and out of the K-O-H as oxytocin levels vary. I add this alternative model to make you think. Much of my hypothesis are open to confirmation and improvements by greater minds than I. This is just a start.

Developing the model:

Like people form like groups: These are suggestions to be validated by the associated groups.

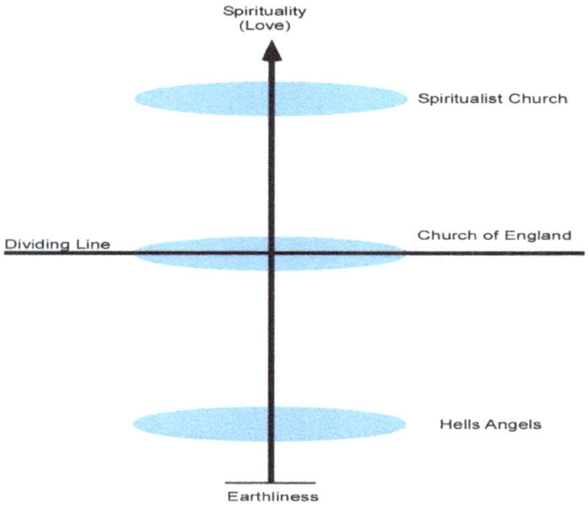

The pigeon-holing is open for interpretation; you may well wish to reallocate specific positions. Positions may change over time too as attitudes change. It serves to illustrate how common groups of peoples sit on the model. I put the Hells angels as earthly because of their love of mechanical machines such as their motorbikes.

Now I propose to extend it to countries:

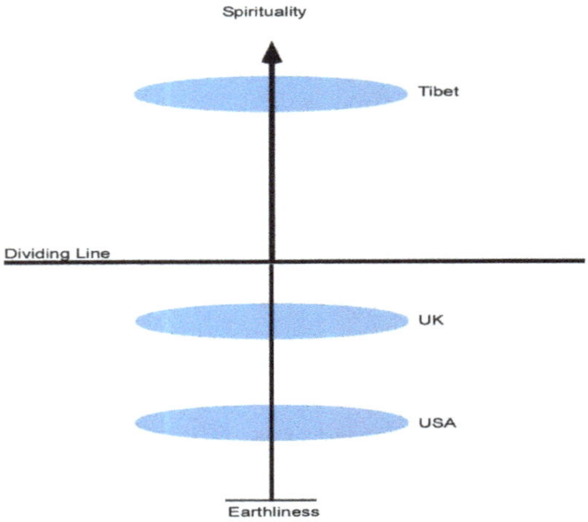

The makeup of the Spirituality or Earthliness of the individuals in each country defines that country's position on the chart. Once again the actual positions are open to discussion particularly the USA as I know many of their population are devotedly religious but USA is also a very materialistic nation.

Another quote from Revelations:

"And I saw a new heaven and earth and the first heaven and the first earth is passed away" Revelations 21:1.

I respectfully assert that my models illustrate the new heaven and earth described.

Revelations refers to a little book. I believe that to be this book. Revelations 10:2, 10:8, 10:9 and 10:10. This book is little as it is all I have to say for now, it is not by design. I didn't relate to the little book mentioned in Revelations until this book was all but completed. If this book is the book of life then everybody is in it, be they Spiritual or Earthly.

I do not profess to understanding the whole of Revelations but the more I re-read it, coupled with current events, the more I understand.

Bryan Adams' song *Heaven* affirms that to be in love is to be in Heaven.

Several songs refer to the power of love, including Jennifer Rush, Huey Lewis and the news and Frankie Goes to Hollywood.

The Kingdom of Heaven and Earthly concept has always been with us. What is different is that I have defined individuals to be one or the other and quantized people's ambient relative positions on that chart.

If people listen and look out for non-verbal gestures for feedback on their behaviour, and act on it, the world would be a far better place.

2.

The Miracles

Despite all of the paranormal experiences I have had they can mostly be explained by coincidence or circumstance. Needless to say I question the biblical miracles of Jesus and could they be explained by using the side effects of love, as previously described, as a key to unlock their meaning. If I could not perform miracles when at my highest, could he?

The virgin birth. The bible was adamant that the virgin was Mary and talks at length of this. But what if the virgin was Jesus himself, being that it was the first time he had been on the planet?

Water to wine. I believe the guests drank water but that JC raised their moods to that of spiritual love and that this was compared to the state of mind induced by drinking fine wine – tipsiness, merriment or outright drunkenness.

Feeding 5000 and 7000. I believe that the crowd brought pack ups of bread and fish to listen to JC preach. Again he elevated their moods to that of spiritual love whereupon their appetites were diminished, as previously described as one of the side effects of love, they ate their fill and gave the remnants to JC to give to those that had brought nothing and still had mounds of food left over.

Walking on water. The only way I can explain walking on water is if you freeze it first. So I believe this parable simply means that JC's feet were extra cold as in the side effects of love described earlier.

Raising the dead. I believe he simply roused Lazarus from a deep coma.

Healing the sick. Healing the sick is the provenance of the medical profession although I do not dispute the power of the mind and body to heal itself. In 100 years' time most illnesses will be eliminated by virtue of the improvements in medical science including gene therapy.

Crucifixion. I do not believe JC was deceased when taken to the tomb but was in a deep coma from which it took some days to come round. When roused his calls from inside the tomb were heard by a number of Earthly guys who freed him from incarceration.

My friend asked the question what made Jesus so special if the miracles were not literal. After much consideration I conclude that it was because he was able to control mental illness. In his day there was no medication for bipolar nor was he liable to be locked up in an asylum.

3.

Fasting

I believe that one has to appreciate cause and effect to understand fasting. When high on love your appetite is diminished and so one can happily exist with a minimal amount of food. If you are not high on love i.e. in the Earthly state then going without food does not produce spirituality it only makes one hungry – ravenous hunger which produces misery. A friend of mine has fasted and commented that you are hungry for the first day, on the second day you lack energy and by the end of the fast you have to force yourself to eat. I still assert that you should not do it unless you are high on love whereupon fasting comes easily and naturally. Jesus is quoted as saying 'do not pull faces to show you are suffering due to fasting'. If you are hungry then you are bound to show your displeasure.

4.

The Hospital Encounter

On one of the latter admissions to a psychiatric ward it has to be said that I was goading one of the patients. I can only remember one of the incidents in which I offered him an extra strong mint from an almost empty packet which he gratefully took and I said take one more for Ron as he went to take another I said lateR ON! After a little more banter he had had enough and set off across the furniture to lump me one. But he had no legs and as he lined up a haymaker of an upper cut, I sank to my knees and offered him a psyche handshake. This he declined in favour of a fist touch and a thumb interlock and the confrontation was defused. I later asked him how he lost his legs and he told me he jumped in front of a train. He was surprised I did not already know but how was I to know without being told?

5.

The Soul, Hell, The Devil, God And Sin

I do not believe in three out of five of these … The soul, hell, the Devil and the verdict is out on the fourth.

A machine as complex as a human brain would invent a soul in order to transcend death. The basic truth is that without a functioning brain there are no thoughts. After death there is nothing, our bodies are variously recycled either into ash when cremated or to return to the earth if buried. This is until our genetic code is replicated by rebirth or in other words reincarnation into a new person. I suggest that in years to come peoples genetic code is used to regenerate people having died. So you may get mothers giving birth to deceased relatives whose DNA has been mapped before they died. This is how the dead will be resurrected.

I believe hell was postulated in order to keep the masses under subjugation. Lead a good life according to the church or you will go to hell.

I do not give credence to the devil despite my purported confrontation with him when I communed with a lightning storm which culminated in the trident of lightning strikes hitting Lincoln cathedral. This was the equivalent of the temptation of Jesus in the wilderness. So I hereby assert that the devil is bound and cast into the bottomless pit for a thousand years as predicted in Revelations 20:2 & 20:3.

My verdict is out on God. If he does not exist who on earth was it that confirmed me as Jesus in that hotel foyer in

Scotland? Who protected me in life threatening situations related in my autobiography? I had once concluded that God was the sum total of love in the universe. I will acknowledge God's existence when he comes to dwell with us on earth as predicted in Revelations 21:3 and I have shaken his hand.

If someone is motivated by love then the world will recognise their endeavours and reward them commensurately such that they will achieve their goals.

I have heard said that there is no design without a designer. But who designed the designer?

Sin. A sin to one person is not a sin to another. To judge one person against your values is not necessarily valid. *"Judge not lest you be judged."* I believe that if you do transgress your values then ill health may well follow. This is not to say that some vices are not reprehensible and should not be committed. For instance a murderer must be taken out of society to eliminate further crimes. To maximise love may be the appropriate mantra.

6.

Global Future

Because the future is foretold in Revelations just maybe it will come true. The time is nigh.

In March 2020 the Covid 19 viruses arrived on our shores. Everything closed for months on end. My cruise was cancelled. My salvation was the Sun newspaper puzzle page. Other newspapers have similar puzzle pages but I like the *Sun*'s. It saved me from climbing the walls during the imposed lockdown. Is Covid the 7 vials released by the angels in Revelations (Revelations 15 onwards)? We have had five variants of Covid to date plus two more recent strains of the last variant. Many more strains may result which the bible does not predict. Also Russia has just invaded Ukraine and Russia is preparing their nuclear arsenal. My interpretation of Armageddon is that it will be the last war and not the end of the world. I have heard that Armageddon is *the last war between good and evil.* Maybe thereafter the world's population can work together for the common good. Revelations 16:16 references Armageddon. It has certainly galvanised me to get this book finished.

A picture of the second coming of the Messiah can be formed from descriptions in Revelations. Firstly he will have a new name. This confirms reincarnation as verified by the fact that we all have a unique DNA which when replicated means reincarnation. However you cannot be reincarnated as the previous incarnation, you are a new person by way of different nature and nature.

In Revelations 1:14 it says that the second coming will have hair as white as snow. This means that he will live long into retirement without being recognised. It also says only he will himself know he was formerly Jesus until outed.

Several times in Revelations it beseeches the churches to listen to the spirit. So clearly the church has it wrong and he reveals the new heaven and earth also predicted in Revelations.

Revelations calls the second coming as being the first and last. This is explained in the model of humanity as Jesus being just above the axis. The first in the kingdom of heaven looking upwards and the last in the kingdom of heaven looking downwards. The church is expecting a super human entity, the highest spiritual being whereas in reality he is the most average man. It is as if they are expecting the child portrayed in the film *The Golden Child* with Eddie Murphy. If this were so he could not remain incognito into his 70th year.

A friend of mine asked am I not worried that I could suffer the same fate all over again. Revelations gives the answer in that *"He that overcometh shall not be hurt on the second death."* Revelations 2:11. His quote is also interesting in that if I had died on the cross my next death would be the third time not the second.

We need space exploration. We cannot sustain an ever increasing population without expanding into space. I believe that if we keep expanding our population exponentially then nature will rebel against us and control our numbers. This has recently been confirmed by the ever increasing average temperature and the resulting severe weather. Maybe Covid is an example of this? As land becomes a premium, war will break out to gain control of it. If nature cannot control us then ultimately human existence will be exterminated.

Until we achieve population of an alternative planet we need to look after our own planet as best we can.

I believe ultimately we are destined to control the universe.

So what do you think … Utter nutter or the real deal?

On A Lighter Note

I have thought up several puns based on classical music:

Which composer doodled a lot? …

Most Art (Mozart)

Which composer of Spartacus and the theme tune to the television show The Onedin Line invariably arrived at his concerts by train? … **Catchachoochootrain (Khachaturian)**

Which composer was no good at pool or snooker but excelled at billiards? …

Rachman-in off (Rachmaninoff)

Which composer was always glad when it was time for bed? …

Rimski Corsetsoff (Rimsky Korsakov)

Which composer was no good at winter sports? …

Tchaich off ski (Tchaikovski)

Which composer liked left over pasta? …

Any O Macaroni (Ennio Morricone)

Which composer was a little daft? …

Sillibalius (Sibalius)

And just to end, a joke told by Barnaby the comedian on a Fred Olson cruise which I have embellished. I did try and let him know but couldn't find a contact for him …

I jostled a guy in the queue for a buffet lunch and he threw a prawn cocktail over me. That's not very nice I said. That's just for starters he said. Next he threw a beef wellington over me. Now you're really putting the boot in I said. Finally he threw the cheese board over my head. That's not very mature I said. Then I said that I was going to report him to the captain and he said don't make a meal out of it. **Boom Boom!**

Personal Future

Who knows what the future holds. I look forward to a few years' time when I can draw my pensions instead of living off my savings. I enjoy cruising which is my preferred holiday.

If things work out and I achieve recognition as the Messiah now that I have delivered the kingdom of heaven I hope I would be able to step up to the job, but would not revel in the adoration the kind of which that the pope receives.

Shortly after going high for the first time I had a premonition that I would have a glass fronted office at an Oxbridge university to teach my ideas and research other religions to incorporate the best parts of them into this new religion. Might this yet come true?

Ingram Content Group UK Ltd.
Milton Keynes UK
UKHW020726070423
419742UK00009B/92

9 781782 229667